S0-AGI-243

# HEALING
## COMMUNITY

# HEALING COMMUNITY

Karin Granberg-Michaelson

## Risk
### BOOK SERIES

WCC Publications, Geneva

Cover design and photo: Rob Lucas

ISBN: 2-8254-1039-X

© 1991 WCC Publications,
150 route de Ferney, 1211 Geneva 2, Switzerland

Risk book series No. 150

Printed in Switzerland

*To Sharon Murfin,*
*partner in ministry,*
*sister in community*

# Contents

# Acknowledgments

I am particularly grateful to David Hilton, M.D., of the Christian Medical Commission, who supported the writing of this book from beginning to end. His careful reading of the manuscript and the questions he raised have greatly strengthened what appears here. Thanks also to my husband, Wesley, for being an advocate in the process of birthing this book.

Many voices have been heard in this book. I am indebted to the Christian Medical Commission for the report *Healing and Wholeness: The Church's Role in Health*, and to several issues of their publication *Contact* for stories of community in other parts of the world. I also thank Dan Kaseje for sharing his personal experience in community; Sharon Murfin, Joe Peterson, Dan Simmons, and Tom King for material about Community Covenant Church; Joe Roos of Sojourners Fellowship; and many other friends who have shared their thoughts, hopes, and dreams about community and healing with me through letters and conversation. To you all I say:

> Let us now depart
> and hold fast to the Covenant,
> knowing that in Christ we are
> no longer strangers and sojourners
> but dearly loved children
> of the living God.

> Mary Gast from
> *No Longer Strangers*

# Preface

We live today in a world that is broken by war, injustice, poverty, exploitation, and ill health. Families, homes, communities, nations, and people are broken. In this world the church has been called to be a healing community.

In this book, Karin Granberg-Michaelson gives us an overview, both personal and general, of actual healing communities, drawing on the experiences of people around the world who have come together to share resources and/or to serve society.

Her own experiences of success and of failure give this book authenticity and relevance for many in the church who are concerned with building healthy communities and want to be agents of change. She also draws on the twelve-year study by the WCC's Christian Medical Commission of health, healing, and wholeness. The findings of this study provide a clear challenge regarding the church on why and how to be involved in a ministry of healing.

This ministry is an integral component of the gospel. We are created to be people in community. Our churches can be revitalized by the awareness that we should seek to become healing communities — to regain a sense of belonging, a common purpose and witness.

As the author says, the early church, as described in Acts, "proclaimed a new order and began to live in one as well." In studying the life, witness, and concerns of that church we may rediscover some essential components of its sense of fellowship and community. The chapter titled "Biblical Origins of Healing Community" can help us to rededicate ourselves to a sense of mission and to a vision of the church as a healing community.

This will not be easy, as we know. We have problems, disappointments, and frustrations in our life together as Christians. We come to appreciate that all of us are wounded, in need of healing, forgiveness, and wholeness. Individually and corporately, Christians will continue to struggle with this reality of brokenness and healing and the discipline and love required to sustain the healing process.

The author is honest about the problems and difficulties of forming healing communities. She has experienced this pain and struggle herself. But this does not mean that we give up or abandon the concept as nothing more than a utopian ideal. Christians have an understanding of the cross that prepares them for the pain and conflict and hope of new life.

There are many disappointments, disillusionments, and even failures in the life of Christian community in a local congregation. Yet it is at this level that we need to work constantly for new expressions of a healing community that has both prophetic and pastoral dimensions, a community with which people can identify. It is to this grassroots community that the message of this book must penetrate — that we *can* work together for healing and wholeness in community life as a local congregation, and thus contribute to the renewal of the church.

This is the excitement and potential of the ministry of healing. For not only does it provide a rationale and vision for what we can do and be in society, but it also gives new meaning to what we can become as church — a community called to bring some harmony, wholeness, *shalom* in this world. That is why this book is so relevant today for local congregations, church leaders, and those concerned with the healing ministry.

Christians must be concerned with the ministry of healing. This book and the work of the WCC's Christian Medical Commission challenge us to rediscover this ministry in our life together and in society.

DR. DALEEP S. MUKARJI
General Secretary
Christian Medical Association of India

# Introduction:
# O Healing River,
# Send Down Your Waters

## In Search of Healing Community within the Church

> We hoped for peace but no good has come,
> for a time of healing but there was only terror.
> Since my people are crushed, I am crushed;
> I mourn, and horror grips me.
> Is there no balm in Gilead?
> Is there no physician there?
> Why then is there no healing
> for the wound of my people?
>
> Jeremiah 8:15, 21–22

During the past thirty years, in the United States and in other parts of the world, there has been a renewed interest in the church as a healing community. Groups of people have come together in many locations, urban and rural, to share their lives closely. This proliferation of new church communities both within and outside denominational structures has had many different aims, but above all they have had a common desire to take the Scripture seriously in everyday life. They have tried to embody New Testament accounts of life in the early church more literally and to respond to the Old Testament injunction to do justice, love mercy, and walk humbly with God. This they have accomplished by a radical sharing of time, money, and spiritual resources.

Most of these church communities are composed of people who are looking for more than average congregational life as we know it in the United States and in Europe. The communities have as their goals to make their faith more real and to have a corporate experience of Christian discipleship. To express their faith more concretely they have formed communities around justice for the poor, witnessing for peace, and health, healing, and wholeness. Elizabeth O'Connor probably said it best when she described the essential commitment of her community, the Church of the Saviour in Washington, D.C., as both a journey inward into one's own interior life with

God and others, and a journey outward that takes the pilgrim into active service or mission in response to human pain.

My own interest in these intentional Christian communities began while I was a short-term missionary in Japan in the early 1970s and very much in search of a faith that seemed more connected to my personal life. I looked for a church where one's own life experience was a valued informer to faith, not overshadowed by scriptural and doctrinal guidance. My interest was also fueled by the conviction that I needed close companions on my journey of faith — that it is not necessary or perhaps even possible to take on a life of Christian discipleship apart from a supportive community of faith in which one can be known, accepted, and challenged to live in faith.

Within the ecumenical community of missionaries gathered in Sendai, Japan, I found the beginning of this new experience of church; I found it as well in a coffeehouse ministry that later grew into a church in Hokkaido, Japan. These experiences formed the inspiration for my studies in theological seminary in Washington, D.C., where I focused on the healing ministry of the church. At the same time, I participated in two remarkable communities of faith and began to experience directly the life and ministry of these two "alternative" churches. Out of the lives of these two churches many concrete expressions of ministry have been born. One such ministry was an inner-city clinic that specialized in a treatment team including a doctor, nurse, pastoral counselor, and social worker to meet the needs of the whole person. Columbia Road Health Services came about through the dream of a few of us, including a physician and me, quickly joined by a nurse practitioner and social worker. The spiritual and physical support of our faith communities, the Church of the Saviour and Sojourners Fellowship, however, is what brought the dream into reality.

In more recent years my experiences with communities of healing have included ten years with a church in Missoula, Montana, which put major energy and vision into being a refuge for many in need of various kinds of healing — physical, emotional, and spiritual. These healing ministries included providing homes for disabled persons, establishing a pastoral counseling center, and responding to many other social needs for healing within the town and the global community. During the same period, our church was part of a network of communities across the United States and had contact with communities in Canada and Europe as well. Representatives from these communities met several times yearly and visited each other's churches to give mutual support and encouragement to persist in trying to live what clearly was an alternative to the way of life in mainstream church and society.

My exploration of healing community was expanded by a working relationship with the Christian Medical College and Hospital in Vellore, south India. On a first visit to the hospital to attend a symposium on Faith and Healing with a gathering of pastors and health and medical professionals from Asia, Africa, and many other parts of the world, I learned that the subject of healing community has been a common interest and a source of fascination to non-Western societies for centuries. It became clear that my own search would be enhanced by a global perspective.

During my seminary studies I became aware of the work of the Christian Medical Commission in Geneva, Switzerland, a program arm of the World Council of Churches. CMC was established in 1968 to give attention to medical missions in the Third World and to examine the role of the church in healing. In India the links between my work and the work of CMC on the issues of health, healing, and wholeness began to grow through exchange with members of CMC's staff who were present at the same symposium. Over the past several years there have been many opportunities to meet with people from all over the world on the subject of healing community. Some of the exchange is based on personal experience within these special communities scattered across the globe. Other exchange reflects a theological or sociological interest in how these communities have come into existence and what is the source of healing power.

Within the communities themselves there have been many changes. Some of the renewal communities that emerged in the 1960s have dwindled in membership or no longer exist, while some of the oldest remain the strongest. This trend is disturbing but not surprising. There have always been examples of renewal movements within the church that flourish and die out. However, the changing shape of community life has caused those who have given themselves to these expressions of the church to question why community is so difficult to sustain. The examples of these faith communities, nevertheless, offer the world church some of the brightest light and hope available for the Christian pilgrim today. Despite their limitations and serious flaws, they are places where healing takes place.

In my own journey I have continued to search for ways to be involved in forming healing community, though my context has shifted to Geneva, Switzerland. How to create a healing community within the international congregation to which I now belong looks very different from the way it did in the more intentional community life that shaped my earlier understanding of what it means to be a healing community in the church. This has taught me that a particular format or location is not as important as finding a way to participate in the healing mission of the church.

The loss of closely knit community life that characterizes many people's lives in all parts of the world today, and the presence of poverty, violence, and war, point to the critical need for healing community. It is the responsibility of the church the world over to be involved in building healing communities — communities that heal both the person and the societies in which we live. These church communities exist everywhere, but they are a small voice that needs to grow stronger and more audible.

The perspective that I bring to this topic will be enriched by voices from various parts of the world church who have thought long and hard on what it means to be a healing community in their context. We urgently need to hear these stories of common struggle to become places of healing in a broken world wherever they are from. For by sharing various experiences with suffering, health, healing, and wholeness, and reflecting on the implications for the whole church, we weave a tapestry of today's salvation history. In this book can be found the personal and the general, the theology and the practice, the hope and the pain of life together. Like others before us, we offer stories of struggle and small victories as a guide to those in search of Christian community and its healing, transforming power.

Any discussion of healing community in the church would not be complete without a general definition of health, healing, and wholeness. From their more than sixty-five-year history in the healing ministry of the church throughout the world, the Roman Catholic order of Medical Mission Sisters offers these descriptions:

- Health in its truest sense is an integration of body, mind and spirit, the self with others; the self and God.

- Healing and health for the whole person involve both preventive and curative medicine; mental and spiritual counseling.

- Wholeness of the person is best achieved by full participation in the community, be it church or local geographical groups.[1]

These observations are borne out by two friends who have each struggled with terminal illness. One friend, describing her treatment for breast cancer, says,

These past eight months have made me even more convinced of the need for wholistic health care — with as much attention paid to mending the wounded spirit as to salvaging the body.... After surgery, chemotherapy, and radiation treatments, there are many times when I feel reduced to being a piece of meat that people do things to. How important Christian communities are at this time, to be the people and place where my humanity and personhood are restored.

Another friend who has struggled daily with a serious and at times life-threatening illness notes:

> I am more convinced than ever that God desires wholeness for my life, but that may not ever mean physical healing. I think it is of more concern to God that I be able to choose and fight for life no matter what.... I'm finding I'm growing in my ability to choose life even in the midst of pain and disease.... And so the journey continues — in many rich new ways I'm finding God and encountering God's healing and love. The physical disease remains an unanswered question.... At times it seems like so much healing happens within me, but what people see is just the continual struggle with the disease — hard to explain.

A Presbyterian pastor expresses the role of the church in the healing ministries this way:

> What does a congregation look like that takes seriously its corporate health and wholeness and that of its members and the community? The church's primary resource in moving people toward health and wholeness is its existence as a fellowship and community. Health is not an individual achievement, but a community responsibility. Only those who share in the brokenness of others are whole.[2]

This discussion of healing community stems from the conviction that we were created by God to live in community. These communities may vary in their reasons for being and they may look different in different areas of the world church. They will surely create pain and brokenness along with the significant healing that takes place. But the core experience of sharing our Christian lives in close community, with all that this implies, is a way of life to be promoted in the church. For me the witness of healing communities throughout the worldwide ecumenical communion is like the tree of life in Revelation, whose leaves are for the healing of nations.

# 1. To Become Healing Communities

## The Christian Medical Commission Challenges the Churches

> Whenever we offer acceptance, love, forgiveness, or a quiet word of hope, we offer health. When we share each other's burdens and joys, we become channels of healing. No matter how timid or tired, selfish or crazy, young or old, we all have something important to offer each other. Each of us is endowed by God with that gift of healing.
>
> — Dr. Eric Ram, director of international health at World Vision

The Christian Medical Commission (CMC) of the World Council of Churches was established in 1968 to promote innovative approaches to health care and the eradication of disease in developing countries, and to assist the church in the search for a Christian understanding of healing and health care. After ten years of successfully promoting community-based health care, CMC was charged to address more fully the needs of the whole person through engaging in theological reflection on the Christian understanding of life, death, suffering, and health. CMC responded to this mandate by holding more than a dozen regional consultations in six continents, the Caribbean, and the Pacific since 1978, in which local pastors, theologians, and medical professionals addressed these questions and tried to outline the church's role in health care.

The purpose of the twelve-year study on health, healing, and wholeness was to discover new thinking on the church's involvement with healing, to become acquainted with healing practices within traditional cultures, to explore ways by which local communities care for their sick, as well as to engage in theological reflection on all aspects of suffering and health.

As the consultations moved from one region to another, new issues emerged. For example, in Central America, the issue of structural injustice and its effect on health was highlighted. In Africa, the issues of traditional healing and African spirituality were central to the discussion of health, healing and wholeness. In Europe, community building was added as an important concern.[3]

But, the major theme expressed in all the consultations was that *health is not primarily medical*. Thus, the majority of health problems in the world cannot be addressed through the increasingly sophisticated health industry. The participants felt that the churches must be called to recognize that the causes of disease are socioeconomic and spiritual as well as bio-medical and to respond by discovering and offering its unique contribution to the promotion of health and well-being.

In 1990, CMC published the findings of its study in a document called *Healing and Wholeness: The Church's Role in Health*. A summary of its findings provides a very clear challenge for the church today as well as concrete suggestions for how the churches can respond. Here is what the regional consultations revealed:

- Health is a justice issue — because poverty is the number one cause of disease. Poverty itself is the result of oppression, exploitation, and war.

- Health is a peace issue — because death due to armed conflict and other political violence is a reality for thousands in a world where torture, imprisonment, and other forms of human rights violations have made wellness of mind, body, and spirit impossible.

- Health is connected to the integrity of creation — in industrialized nations, where modernization has introduced addicting drugs, new diets, and disdain for manual labor, as much as 80 percent of illness and death is due to self-inflicted destructive lifestyles.

  Nuclear waste and pollution produced by material greed and the struggle for national supremacy are threatening the health of the planet itself.

- Health is a spiritual issue — those in loving harmony with God and neighbor not only survive tragedy best whatever their economic situation, but grow stronger in the process. Not only does the Christian gospel speak directly to the spiritual reality of health, but salvation through Christ is healing.

Our body/mind/spirit can be broken by social injustice, misuse of power, unhealthy relationships and lifestyle, lack of care for and abuse of the creation, individualism, materialism, and false spirituality. Many people needlessly suffer. At times it seems that some people are born without any choice but to suffer. But our encounter with Jesus Christ, the healer, reminds us that the meaning and purpose of life are found in our ongoing struggle with the powers that deny God's gift of life. This is a message for both the rich and poor.[4]

The church can respond to the overwhelming need for wholeness in our world by being involved with organizations that empower communities who are fighting for health, human rights, and liberation. In this way we can fight the powers that deny God's gift of life. The church can read the Bible with new eyes that lead to entering into the life and experience of the poor. Together, we can form healing communities where the cries of all people are heard and responded to.

The former general secretary of the World Council of Churches, Dr. Philip Potter, summarized the healing impact of participating with the poor in their struggle for justice and liberation:

In many parts of the world Christians, in their struggle for justice and human rights, have discovered that within the struggle, as they expose the evils around them with the living word of God, and as they express their costly solidarity with the oppressed, they are given new and refreshing access to the healing power of God. They are brought closer to the healing presence of God in prayer and praise, in authenticity and wholeness. Despair and death have no longer any power over them. They have already tasted the risen life of Christ and so have become ministers of God's healing, life-sustaining grace in the midst of the sicknesses of our world. That is what we have been learning from our various contact groups, the base communities, the many persons and action groups who are subjected to imprisonment, torture and death because of their witness to the health — wholeness — which God offers in broken, bleeding societies.[5]

## The Role of the Community

It is in the context of community with God, with life, and with creation that we experience both our brokenness and what we know of wholeness.

A true community is not closed. It cuts across class, status and power structures. Its members must risk moving out to identify with the people who are on the fringes, inviting the marginalized and oppressed in, enabling them to rejoin their communities with restored relationships. It is a life-giving organism with movement in and out which gives rise to new communities of healing and fellowship.

As one body with different parts, we cannot have true community unless each of us shares in its life — placing our talents at the service of others. When one suffers, all suffer, when one receives honor all rejoice together. When one part of the community is in pain, the whole body groans. When one part is healed, the whole body is renewed. It is not right for some parts of the body to be feeling well while other parts of the same body are suffering.[6]

Many congregations have not developed mechanisms to care for their members. So, as with the lunatic man of Gadara, the response is to get rid of the problem by excommunicating or isolating sick persons instead of coming to their rescue and restoring their life in the community. In all regions the study revealed how important it is for each member of the congregation to contribute to the healing mission of the church.[7]

In many of the regional consultations CMC learned that people in the churches are actively engaged in healing through the laying on of hands, prayer, anointing the sick with oil, caring for people by providing food and medicine, and visiting the sick at home or in hospitals. These activities are not to be set in opposition with medical science, which God also uses to heal people. Among the practices that can aid in healing are scientific medicine, traditional medicine, alternative forms of medicine, prayer, meditation, and liturgy. Each, especially when coupled with faith, can provide healing.[8]

In the Egyptian Consultation held in Alexandria in 1980, participants shared:

> Healing and the building of community, according to the Orthodox view, are part of the basic concepts of forgiveness and the Eucharist. The final concept of forgiveness is the restoration of a person to the community. It is this concept that lies behind the pronunciation of the absolution in the Orthodox church, an absolution addressed not to a singular but to a plural object and repeated not once but several times in the liturgy. Why? Because sin shatters the community and forgiveness restores healthy relationships within the community.
>
> At present, we are facing the disintegration of the Christian dogmas of forgiveness and the church of God, partly because we are not aware that we are members of a community, partly because we are no longer taking forgiveness seriously as the healing of the soul and body, partly because confession has become a mechanical process.
>
> The divine grace that is received in the sacrament of the Eucharist is indeed the divine power that makes us all one body.... This is the true understanding that when I receive the Eucharist, I receive also the responsibility of the life, sickness and health of those who partake with me of the divine sacrifice.[9]

The Orthodox view that we are all participating in a community to which we are bound through the Eucharist in the life, death, and resurrection of Jesus Christ is a valuable reminder to the world church today. In some Orthodox communities it has been the practice to make public confession of sin before receiving the sacraments in the Eucharist. This confession then led to public forgiveness and absolution — wiping the slate clean as a person was restored to the community. Perhaps we will never fully understand the healing effects of confession and forgiveness and restoration to the community on the immune system of the body. But as a church we must hold fast to this insight preserved in most traditional societies even today. This connection between attitudes and feelings — living in a state of grace — and our health is underscored by cancer surgeon and author Bernie Siegel in his recent book *Love, Medicine and Miracles*. He says that, "Unconditional love is the most powerful stimulant of the immune system. The truth is: love heals."[10]

Dr. Abraham Verghese, professor of psychiatry at the Christian Medical College and Hospital in Vellore, India, sees restoration to the community as a key issue in the recovery of the psychiatric patients he treats. His treatment plan relies on family participation and presence throughout all stages of mental illness. Families live with the patient during hospitalization, and they participate in groups in which they learn more about the nature of the illness their loved one is suffering and, perhaps more importantly, how to restore their family member to the larger village community, where persons who suffer psychiatric disorders are stigmatized and isolated. Dr. Verghese sees a role for the Christian congregation in restoring a previously sick person to the community:

> Christian faith is the good news of the recovery of the wholeness of persons and reconciliation of the human community as revealed in Christ. The imperative of the gospel is to appropriate for ourselves and mediate for others this healing power of Christ. Local congregations should recognize the healing function as part of the total ministry of the church and function as healing communities.
>
> The Church should be a fellowship of love, showing loving concern for others which will be an incentive for healing. It should be a fellowship of worship, emphasizing the reality of God as revealed in Christ, which through the ministry of word and sacrament will bring people into healing contact with God. It should be a fellowship of reconciliation, eliminating needless social and psychological tensions. It should be a fellowship of prayer, for prayer is a healing force.[11]

### Questions for the Churches

The question for each local church to pursue is how to become a healing community. Some of the resources available identified by CMC after more than twelve years of intensive study, dialogue, and fact-finding include:

*Church-based Activities:*

- Bible study on health, healing, and wholeness
- Praying for the sick
- Confession and forgiveness
- Laying on of hands
- Anointing with oil
- Holy communion
- Celebrating healing liturgies
- Using charismatic gifts

*Primary Health Care Education:*

- Medical intervention
- Training healers
- Cooperating with other healing partners
- Supporting those in healing ministries
- Providing health education
- Facilitating self-discovery of causes for ill-health

*Justice and Advocacy:*

- Learning to take personal responsibility for health
- Studying questions of medical ethics
- Learning to see health as a justice issue
- Advocating the elimination of poverty and oppression
- Supporting the struggle of people seeking liberation from all forms of injustice

As with any matter that is vitally important to the well-being of many, there will always be more questions than answers about how to create healing community within the church. It seems appropriate to conclude this mandate by sharing the questions CMC has been raising during its study on health, healing, and wholeness so that as the church moves to respond to the critical needs for healing community we may also learn, in Rilke's words, to be patient and to try to love the questions themselves:

- Are we and our churches healing communities?

- Are we really engaging ourselves in God's controversy with those who spread sickness around?

- Are we enabling our sick people and societies to diagnose their true sickness and find resources for healing?

- Are we prepared to place ourselves beside the sick, the deprived, the oppressed with the healing power of God?

- Are we ready to join our Lord in his self-giving struggle with evil even to the cross in order that healing, reconciliation, and wholeness may become manifest in a world which is sick unto death?

Finally, how do we answer these questions? It would seem that the questions themselves require a community context in which to pursue the solutions. In the act of creating a caring community one finds that the community has become a place of healing. In the Budapest Consultation held in 1986, a group report affirmed:

> It is clear to us that care of those who are sick or suffering is not a matter for just the doctor alone, but for everyone connected with that person. What is needed is a willingness on the part of all of us to enter into a deeper relationship, to talk and take counsel together, from which we can draw strength — the sense of bearing one another's burdens.

The need to build healing communities emerged as a theme throughout all the regional gatherings convened by CMC:

> People are lonely, empty and feel alienated because of growing individualism and materialism, not only from developed nations but developing nations who have lost

15

their sense of community. The church is challenged to teach its members to care for each other, to confess their sins and brokenness, to nurture the unique contribution each can make, and thereby to model for the world the health, healing and wholeness which is the promise of God.[12]

Can the church do less than to accept this challenge?

# 2. Healing Community in Global Perspective

> Then the angel showed me the river of the water of life, as clear as crystal, flowing from the throne of God and of the Lamb down the middle of the street of the city. On each side of the river stood the tree of life, bearing twelve crops of fruit, yielding its fruit every month. And the leaves of the tree are for the healing of the nations. No longer will there be any curse.
>
> — Revelation 22:1–3

Imagine a tree of life whose leaves contain the secret to heal the nations — a tree that bears monthly crops according to the season, a tree watered by a river that flows from the very throne of God in Christ. In that picture is the possibility for God's new order in the new Jerusalem where the curse has been removed and *shalom* restored. This metaphor also contains a seed of truth that can guide the church right now as it seeks to discover and live in God's new order. For churches on their way to becoming healing communities are like the tree of life whose leaves are for the healing of the nations. A healthy tree has many leaves and the church expresses its healing mission in many ways. The variety of healing communities at work in the world today resembles the rotating monthly crops provided by the tree of life. The image of the tree of life is a powerful reminder of the global healing mission to which the whole church is called.

This discussion of healing community is rooted in the belief that it is a global and ecumenical reality. While communities may have different visions and ways of working together to accomplish their mission, ultimately they all exist for the healing of the nations. Healing communities from the North and South need each other to find the wholeness God intends for us all. It is obvious that communities in the developing countries are forced to concentrate on practical survival needs, while those in the more developed nations may have the luxury to focus on theological, ethical, and philosophical issues. The division between rich and poor is in the end perhaps more powerful than the divisions of race and sex. The developed nations, too, have their pockets of poverty where people starve in the midst of plenty. This division between rich and poor certainly creates different kinds of communities in different corners of the world. Yet they are all needed because the Body has many parts and each is indispensable to the other. In 1 Corinthians Paul says that in fact we cannot exist without each other.

This call for interdependence is very different from the reality most of us know. We have separated ourselves from this reality in the world today. The North in fact is arrogant and cannot imagine what it needs to learn from the experience of the poor in traditional cultures of the South. Yet it is in the cries of the people for liberation from all forms of injustice that we are all awakened to the vision of the reign of God and the need for the church to respond in a peaceful revolution so that righteousness and peace at last will join hands.

The contribution of South to North is contained in part by the liberation theology that comes from Latin America and is echoed in Asian and African experiences of political repression. In these regions the people of God have come together in ecclesial base communities to say no to death and disorder and to build communities of hope that read and interpret the Bible with new eyes — the eyes of wounded healers. The Bible they read together instructs them to rise up and be free from all that is holding them back. These communities of liberation are sounding a call to the rest of the church to respond to the cries of all people. But what does the South have to teach the North about creating healing communities? And how can this dialogue take place?

The Christian Medical Commission of the World Council of Churches has learned that traditional societies have an inherent understanding of health that knows that disturbances in beliefs and feelings are root causes of illness. Many of these societies have preserved the sense of belonging to the community that the developed nations have lost or are in danger of losing. The sense of identity and place provided by traditional cultures protects individuals against the feelings of isolation and alienation that are a bitter reality for many living in industrialized nations of the North. Even though progress is a comfortable disease that has spread the sickness of the modern age throughout all the world's cities, traditional societies do not so quickly succumb to the breakdown of life in community.

The church needs to take hold of this message that we were created to be people in community — not isolated individuals pursuing our own futures. Traditional concepts of health and sickness support the view that disharmony in relationships with God, neighbor, and significant relatives leads to separation, brokenness and sin. This lack of well-being occurs in all cultures and calls for gifts the church has to offer. Confession and forgiveness restore a person to life in community. In Africa and Asia, the family or a community elder deal with broken relationships.

Not only can much be learned from a dialogue between traditional healers and Western medical practitioners, but the church can learn from these traditional models of caring community. Things might look very different in many churches in the North if elders in the community saw it as their responsibility to mediate troubled relationships. In many parts of the North, particularly in large cities, the heritage of being part of something larger than oneself has been lost. There is no community and there is no longer an elder with the authority to bring wounded parties together to seek reconciliation. Pastors who are themselves isolated and alienated cannot create community out of nothing and are not prepared in many cases to intervene in the lives of people in their congregation.

In one such church two couples who had been close friends experienced a sudden break in the relationship. The person who broke off the friendship would not explain what had gone wrong. Nor would he respond when the others tried to mend things. After much prayer and reflection, another church member and friend to them all went to their pastor and asked for help in mediat-

ing the situation. The pastor didn't want to get involved.
These people, all committed Christians, are still not reconciled after many years have passed. Unfortunately,
every church and every person have broken relationships
that spoil the unity and harmony in which Christians are
called to live. This disharmony should not be allowed to
continue, but many congregations lack both the sense of
belonging and the support that is needed to be reconciled
with one another.

Those in the North have moved far away from their
roots in earlier traditional communities where people
knew where they came from and to whom they belonged.
It is no wonder then that so much of the disease prevalent
in affluent societies represents disorder of the soul and
stems from this lack of community. Although communities in the South struggle against seemingly insurmountable obstacles of poverty, disease, and war, many have
preserved a sense of belonging that promotes well-being
and combats illness.

## The East African Revival

What do these communities look like and how can
the whole church benefit from their example? Do they
bear any resemblance to the community experience of
the North?

Dan Kasege, director of the Christian Medical Commission of the WCC, comes out of a community experience in his home of Kenya. He and his family participated
in the East African Revival (EAR), which swept the country in the early 1930s and 1940s and still exists in a
modified form today. The East African Revival began in
Rwanda, but it quickly spread throughout the whole of
East Africa. Initially, the revival was a threat to the or-
ganized church, but eventually many pastors joined in,
and in this way its impact was felt by the mainstream of
the East African church. Like other renewal movements
within the church the EAR has faced the challenges of
providing leadership in a changing world. Today it exists
in four camps with differing emphases.

The EAR was centered around personal conversion and giving public witness to that experience. There was a very specific way in which people shared their testimony with one another. The language used was an immediate point of identification with strangers who shared the same experience. People would greet each other by saying, "I'm Dan, I'm a sinner, but the Lord spoke to me and I went to the cross where I was washed in the blood. Since that time, I am still walking by repentance and forgiveness with the Lord."

In Dan's view, the outstanding gift of this revival was the way in which the Scripture was applied in the local context where it was being shared. Each Bible study meeting would lead the group to a specific form of response, particularly to needed repentance or confession. People would then seek to restore the broken relationship on the spot.

General themes were developed and became mottos by which the group lived. One such theme was centered on the phrase, "I am satisfied," and was meant to imply that Jesus is the basis for genuine satisfaction, whatever a person's social or economic circumstances.

Repentance was central to maintaining what was called their "walk in the light." Members felt a constant need to put right their relationship with God and others. What this meant to participants in the revival was what they called a repeated "journey to the cross" to make confession and be restored in fellowship. The repeated self-examination meant that people had a strong sense of personal responsibility for their faith and did not tend to blame others for their failures. They also took personal responsibility for being reconciled with others in the community when things became amiss.

Within this community, Dan began and ended his day with times of fellowship that included public confession of wrongdoing. As a teenager this was sometimes difficult, but today he recognizes the merit of this practice and sees potential for its use in the larger church. "Walking in the light" was a call to be transparent in one's relationships, including sharing thoughts, decisions, and whatever of importance was happening in one's life. The worship always included praising God, reflecting on the Bible, prayer, and testimonies of how the Scripture had spoken to individuals.

The EAR community gathered frequently. In mid-week they met for Bible study and testimonies, several congregations would gather weekly for worship, monthly meetings were held with an even larger group of parishes, and yearly the revival held a convention. The connection to one another was maintained not primarily through living close together, but through shared testimony. When members heard of fellow members traveling through their region, they would go to meet their train with food and songs of praise. Although not a dominant characteristic of the East African Revival movement, healings were sometimes the result of such transparent living in community.

What can the world church learn from the East African Revival's attempt to be a healing community? Dan Kasege believes the lessons include the prominence of confession and forgiveness combined with the deep sense of solidarity and mutual support within the community. The encouragement to "be broken" or humble oneself in a dispute, rather than insisting on one's own way, could lead all of us to greater unity and wholeness. Additionally, the challenge to be transparent and walk in the light with self, neighbor, and God calls the church back to its origins described in Acts and the epistles.

Dan's personal experience in community has two dimensions — that of his Christian formation in the East African Revival and his experience of community in his extended family. He believes that the breakdown of community life is also at work in the South to the detriment of people's health and sense of well-being. The role of the extended family is being diminished and relegated to ritual events like marriage, births, and deaths, as adult children scorn traditional values and leave home, breaking off ties with their community of origin.

The elderly parents who are left behind often become caught between the community they know and are a part of, and the new world their children inhabit in faraway countries. The separation causes stress and illnesses to both generations. At present, Dan is studying the effects of this separation and seeing that people have been struck with illnesses that would previously have been unknown in their culture. He is also investigating what happens to people who leave the village community for the city but remain in Africa, and those who leave their community and their country, like himself. A marked increase in hypertension is only one of the symptoms Dan has discovered resulting from the pain of separation from the community. As the extended family breaks down throughout the world, Dan thinks the church can be the alternative extended family.

### The Base Communities

The ecclesial base community movement of Latin America is another model of healing community that can enrich the world church. The base communities, which are a major force in the remarkable political change taking place today, are the direct result of people empowered by faith and community that comes directly out of their experiences with poverty and political injustice. As theologian Jürgen Moltmann has said, those who read the Bible on an empty stomach draw conclusions different from those who are reading it in comfortable surroundings. Reading the Bible from the perspective of life in the *favelas* or *barrios pobres* in countries where the debt crisis primarily affects the poor — who are already groaning under the burdens of hunger, malnutrition, illiteracy, and political violence — has created new communities that are shaping a grassroots theology that is influencing the ecumenical church.

Two North American pastors I know well have been profoundly influenced by the similarities of the struggle of the urban poor in the North American city in which they live and work and the ecclesial base communities they have been visiting on a regular basis during the past five years. After a recent visit they each wrote their reflections. Bruce Menning wrote on the base communities he has visited in Latin America, and Gene Beerens wrote about the base community he is experiencing with ex-prisoners in the inner city where he ministers.

Bruce calls the base communities a New Reformation in the church — a living sign that our theology must lead to political and economic action. He suggests that the poor see God most clearly because they have fewer idols than the rich. This should lead the church to trust what the poor say about God and to be suspicious of how the rich use God to defend the status quo. In Bruce's own words:

> There is a conversion that comes from non-tourist travel to the third world countries. It challenges one's theology, ecclesiology, politics, economics and lifestyle.... The word of God has been rediscovered by the people. They have claimed it as their possession, both in its reading and its interpretation. It ties all of life together and gives it meaning. Furthermore, the scripture has called forth a priesthood of all believers, producing leadership for church and society. Pope John XXIII sought a church that was more than hierarchy. He sought a church actively made up of the whole people of God. Nowhere is this vision of the church more clearly realized than in the base communities.[13]

Sociologist Jether Pereira Ramalho of Brazil says that the church base communities represent the search for a new way of being the church. They are a model of church community where there is not a hierarchy of power, but an emphasis on equal participation of all elements of the community. The base communities are pledged not only to the renewal of the church but to building a more just and egalitarian society. Although the base communities began in the Roman Catholic church, many Protestant congregations are following their example. Base communities are not limited to Brazil or even to Latin America, but have sprung up in Asia and Africa wherever people are taking their faith into their own hands.[14]

The Bible is being studied within the social context of the community with the participation of all. Since 1975 there have been seven inter-church gatherings where base communities have shared their experiences with one another. In a workshop on the popular reading of the Bible held in Chile, a priest observed: "Whenever a group of oppressed people become aware of their situation and join together in a practical effort for their own liberation, the spirit of the risen Christ is present supporting and strengthening his people." The base communities are stretching the people to be involved with issues they would otherwise avoid.[15]

At a gathering of women from the base communities of São Paulo, Bruce and Gene shared in a creative liturgy that noted the ways in which women and children are crucified in society and celebrated the promise of their resurrection. They observed that the community of women is also developing solidarity with prostitutes, who have been forced into their trade for survival. For them religious commitment leads to political involvement.

Base community gatherings may be planned by a nun or priest, but there is strong lay participation. Small groups come together informally to pray, read the Bible, and apply it to their own life situation. They take time to share their insights with one another. Brazilian Lutheran theologian Wanda Deifelt says that biblical texts are often used as a background to analyze common problems the community faces, such as poor housing conditions and lack of drinking water. In this way, Christian faith is being translated into the everyday reality of poor people. For many of the women involved in the church base communities, Bible study has been the first step toward self-awareness that has led them to become active in political issues outside the church as well.[16]

Sr. Anne Moran, who is involved in a base community on the periphery of São Paulo, believes that at their best base communities are centers of unity that express the tremendous power of unified effort, camaraderie, and mutual support. One of the themes she observes in the base communities is that reflection must lead to action, that it is important to be involved with making life better for all rather than remaining a passive bystander. Another is a theme that has been explored by Christian communities the world over, namely trust. As people in the base communities come to know and trust each other, the Scripture comes alive in their sharing. Those with the courage to share their needs find that in time of need the community is there. They are not alone.[17]

Describing the journey of the Medical Mission Sisters, who have been involved in the healing ministry of the church for over sixty-five years, Sarah Summers and Mary Pawath report that they began to sense a call to create caring communities in which people became aware of their own right to life and health. Their programs became more community based and the people themselves began to identify needs and make decisions about responses. "We knew that we could no longer remain silent in the face of unjust local, national, and international systems and policies that affected life and health."[18]

This has led the Medical Mission Sisters to move into public life and to help the people they are working with exert pressure on government hospitals in the Philippines and in south India to provide accessible health care. They note that they are learning again and again that the process of healing is essentially one of building relationships and so building one world. "Healing is a way of life in which all of us recognize that our humanness is being drawn by God into wholeness," they write. Catholic priest Thomas Merton said that "the whole idea of compassion is based on a keen awareness of the interdependence of all living beings which are all part of one another and all involved in one another."[19] The Medical Mission Sisters are convinced that a context of mutuality and interdependence, such as in the base communities they are working with in Latin America, the Philippines, and India, promotes health, healing, and wholeness.

Christian Reformed pastor Gene Beerens's several trips to Latin America to dialogue with base community leadership caused him to make many comparisons to his own ministry with recently released prisoners in inner-city Grand Rapids, Michigan. In his reflections, which he titled "Liberation of Captives Closer to Home," Gene notes that the Third World exists in the First World and vice versa in any context where people are held hostage to injustice by their national and cultural systems. This insight has challenged him to participate in a form of Christian base community among the volunteer staff and ex-prisoners with whom he works. Gene finds that the weekly support group has challenged his assumptions and values and empowered his formerly imprisoned sisters and brothers who are trying to re-enter North American society.

The growing base community will soon "multiply by division." Gene finds that the small percentage of people who have chosen to be part of this group are all being converted and rehabilitated. In adapting many principles of the base communities of Latin America to his own inner city context in the U.S., Gene is demonstrating what our churches could do on a larger scale to share ways of forming communities where all forms of healing — physical, emotional, spiritual, and societal — can take place. The Cross Road Correctional Ministries has identified the following results from their Bible study, fellowship, and prayer together, which can be useful to all of us seeking to integrate the ecumenical gleanings of the churches of South and North:

- Bible study and reflection on its application in our individual contexts have led to greater awareness and deeper analysis of the societal roots of problems which members have experienced.

- By encouraging full participation of everyone and rotating the leadership of the group, each member's sense of dignity and self-worth has grown and their various gifts are being discovered and developed.

- As dignity is restored and abilities are affirmed, people begin to affirm responsibility for their lives and enter into healthier relationships.

- Within the group members begin to trust one another and form bonds of Christian community so they can address their common concerns and the conditions that have deprived them of their dignity.

- Continuing conversion and growth take place within this communion as members encounter the word of God together and work and pray together.

- In the context of mutual respect and trust members are able to evaluate and develop the whole ministry as it serves other former prisoners and they are also able to sensitize and train those who volunteer for service.

- As members discuss together the changes needed in the criminal justice system, plans of action are formulated and individuals are prepared for education and advocacy work.

- As gifts for ministry are discovered, members are able to share in ministry to others still in prison or newly released, and to speak to the larger Christian community about the challenge and necessity of this ministry.

- As members return to the group, experiences in advocacy and ministry are shared for encouragement or for further advice and insights.

- A network is forming with other area groups which engage in peace and justice activities, for example, an alternative celebration of a public holiday which discriminates against Native Americans, including confession and seeking reconciliation with those who are members of our community.[20]

In summary, Gene says,

It is not only the prisoner or former prisoner who needs to hear the forgiving and liberating gospel of Jesus Christ. We as well need to hear it — from their unique vantage point — as it impacts that "space" where structural evil and personal sin have deeply entangled and damaged so many lives. Perhaps they have more to offer to us than we to them, if we really care to learn about how the demons and idols of sin and death affect us all.[21]

## Traditional Wisdom

In another corner of the world, Dr. Benjamin Pulimood, director of the Christian Medical College and Hospital in Vellore, describes how some Indian Christians have adapted the wisdom of their indigenous religious traditions to the creation of Christian ashrams. These ashrams, located all over India, promote healing community by encouraging their members to practice a simple lifestyle focused on the Spirit. Members live in simple facilities and create an atmosphere of tranquility through daily prayer and devotion. Counseling or spiritual direction is provided by experienced members. The ashram community seeks to develop an attitude of detachment that frees them from the distractions of life, allows them to concentrate on communing with God, and reflects their multi-faith roots.[22]

Some Christian medical institutions in India, like the college and hospital in Vellore, are making use of the ashram principles in the treatment of medical patients. Reverend A. C. Oomen, former hospital chaplain at Vellore, writes of his experience:

> In almost every aspect of healing recorded in the New Testament, there is a community present either bringing the patient to the Lord, or coming with the healer. Health is far from individualistic. It is realized in relationship.... Nearly every disease described in the New Testament has a symbolic value as the disease of the community. The blind man points out those who cannot see the truth, the deaf, those who are insensitive to the voice of God. To forget this representative aspect both of sickness and of health is to miss the centrality of the meaning of the *koinonia* in the New Testament.[23]

Sister Mary MacDonald, a member of a Melanesian pastoral and socioeconomic institute in Papua New

Guinea, describes healing in the community of the South Kewa people by saying:

> As for the people of Jesus' time, so too for the people of Mararoko today, sickness is viewed in terms of damaged or broken relationships, in terms of sinfulness. Traditional society provides for confession of sins on occasions of illness and danger of death, and a preliminary task for healers is to discover what wrongdoing or broken relationship of the sick person or his or her family has caused the illness. This may be openly confessed or suggestions or accusations may be made. The "damage" must be recognized and put right so that the sick person can be restored to health and reconciled to his or her community.[24]

Using their own traditional healers and Western nurses, the people of Mararoko anoint their sick with oil and employ the laying on of hands. In some cases the traditional healers may even choose to anoint the whole body of the sick person.

One can find many such examples of healing community and healing practices throughout the globe. What is important is that the churches recognize the common thread in these examples and consider them carefully as they continue to pursue their healing mandate:

- People belong in community whether it is to be found in the extended family or in the church.

- Community and a sense of belonging significantly impact health.

- Reconciliation within community life always creates wholeness and sometimes even cure.

- Finding one's place and experiencing solidarity in the struggle for justice and liberation are empowering and thus healing.

- All communities require commitment and self-sacrifice whatever their context.

# 3. Biblical Origins
##   of Healing Community

> They devoted themselves to the apostles' teaching and fellowship, to the breaking of bread and the prayers. Awe came upon everyone, because many wonders and signs were being done by the apostles. All who believed were together and had all things in common; they would sell their possessions and goods and distribute the proceeds to all, as any had need. Day by day, as they spent much time together in the temple, they broke bread at home and ate their food with glad and generous hearts, praising God and having the goodwill of all the people. And day by day the Lord added to their number those who were being saved.
>
> — Acts 2:42–47

It is always simpler to describe what is needed than to create it. Every church can become a healing community, but to do so requires a new understanding of what it means to be the church. Many churches throughout the world today have lost the vision held by the early church as it is described in the Acts of the Apostles. They appear to have more in common with government bureaucracies than with the new family described in Acts and in the Pauline epistles. Although the Scriptures must always be reinterpreted in the context in which we live, we can find in them vivid description and teaching about life together. So the church would do well to reconsider the testimony of the early church as it seeks to build healing communities in today's world.

The early church described in Acts had a very clear vision of its purpose. It understood its primary function to be that of witness and proclamation of the good news of Jesus Christ. Members enacted their commitment through a radical sharing of their economic resources with one another and the poor. They also devoted much time to prayer, fasting, preaching, healing, and corporate acts of worship. In the process of committing their lives to a common purpose and following this sense of calling together, the lives of the membership were transformed. They proclaimed a new order and they began to live in one as well.

> Now the whole group of those who believed were of one heart and soul, and no one claimed private ownership of any possessions, but everything they owned was held in common. With great power the apostles gave their testimony to the resurrection of the Lord Jesus, and great grace was upon them all. There was not a needy person among them. (Acts 4:32–34)

The requirements for membership in the early church were also very clear and uncompromised. Members had to believe in the life, death, and resurrection of Christ. They had to repent from their former life and to undergo the ritual of water baptism. Baptism symbolized the death of the old and beginning of a new life in Christ. At Pentecost, the early church community had the experience of being empowered by the Holy Spirit for ministry in a new way. Out of this dramatic experience of empowerment through the Holy Spirit, they began to develop an understanding of spiritual gifts and their place in the community's life.

Strong leadership played an important role in the life of the early church through the ministry of Peter followed by Paul and Barnabas. These men were understood by the members as having been chosen by God, and they exercised a particular authority in the community's life. Theirs was a servant leadership not based in power over others, but in following Jesus' example of taking the form of a servant (Phil. 2:5–11). It is important to note in terms of contemporary struggles over clergy and lay leadership as well as the role of women in leadership of the community that although there was strong leadership, it was shared among the twelve apostles and later with many others, including women like Priscilla. Clearly, the early church's guide for determining its leaders was based on a manifestation of spiritual gifts exercised on behalf of the community's good.

The New Testament also reveals that the early church adopted strict moral norms and that whenever these were abandoned, the community life began to disintegrate. But the outstanding characteristic of the early church was its commitment to the community as the context in which to express their belief in Christ. In fact, persecution and trials seem only to have intensified the loyalty of most of the members.

### Creating Communities Today

What do these attributes of the early church's life tell us about creating healing communities within the contemporary church?

It is the communal dimension of the early church, the fellowship of the beloved disciples, that I believe can be most instructive as we attempt to build healing communities in our churches today. Christian community is based on the same *koinonia* fellowship. As Roman Catholic theologian Gabriel Moran has said, "Community means that by meeting another person at the level of our common humanity we will share the affection and encouragement, sympathy and intimacy, the truth and the love that will enable us to become more wholly and integrally ourselves."[25] At its best, the community is a group that provides support, consolation, security, intimacy, moral depth, social cohesion, and continuity.

But Christian community is more than personally empowering: it must lead the way to God's intended order. The early church had a vision that extended beyond itself. Communities that succeed in their life together do not exist merely for themselves but for the purpose of bringing God's new reign to the world in which we are living. The community is bound by the mandate of creating justice wherever injustice is present through the giving of its time, money, and personal sacrifice. In a healing community one is challenged to internalize the Magnificat of Mary, which was echoed by Jesus in words much like this paraphrase that I found recently:

> God has chosen ME and sent ME to bring good news to the poor, to heal the brokenhearted, to announce release to captives and freedom to those in prison. God has sent ME to proclaim that the time has come when God will save the people.[26]

The early church had a common vision of justice and mercy. Healing communities today are still bound together by faith in a common vision of God's purposes in the world. As Stephen Clark, author of *Building Christian Communities*, writes, "The main goal of pastoral efforts in the church today is to build communities which make it possible for a person to live a Christian life." Most churches fail to empower members for this ministry by failing to provide structures that allow people to spend enough significant time together. Significant time implies time spent developing relationships based on mutual commitment to finding God's purposes for oneself and for the community as a whole. That is why churches that spend most of their time on administrative detail eliminate the necessary additional time and energy to build something lasting together.

Forming community requires a commitment to spending a great deal of time together in work, play, and worship. It is the kind of time one spends with a lover, because it must eventually include intimate exchanges of trust. This experience of intimacy required to create a healing community cannot happen through a weekly service that is filled with sermon and liturgy, as important as they are to the church's life. It takes time to draw people into a vision of the church as large as the early church's was. Without such a vision the people perish, which is exactly the plight of many churches in the world today. They lack a compelling vision of healing and justice.

Building healing communities is also an act of obedience to God, according to Father Richard Rohr, founder of the New Jerusalem Community in the United States. Rohr says that "every attempt at faith community is participation in the eternal longing of God that we might be one."[27] He also says that Jesus' mission and the purpose of the church center on learning to become a spiritual family or community. For Father Rohr, if we learn to have real fellowship with one another, then mission and the spreading of the good news will follow. There is a precedent for this understanding in the Old Testament account of the calling of the prophet Isaiah. Christ himself called a small group together, lived among his brothers and sisters, and performed his mission in their company. Christ also sent people out in mission by twos, which indicates the value of spiritual companionship.

Fellowship means living our lives in Christ in openness with one another. As Dietrich Bonhoeffer wrote in *Life Together*, "It is in confession that the breakthrough to community takes place." There is no hiding in healing community. One must learn to accept the discipline of self-disclosure to receive fully the sacrament of forgiveness. No one is righteous, not one, the Scripture reminds us. But we are so schooled in self-protection that it requires an act of faith to reveal ourselves as we really are behind the idealized images. Confessing who we are not frees everyone in the community from the yoke of perfectionism, which blocks us from receiving grace and forgiveness. What we have to give to another is our commitment to struggle in faith and our intention to forgive another as we have been forgiven. We need and long for this kind of healing so that we can all move into the works of justice and mercy God has given everyone in every time and in every place to do.

It takes constant recommitment to build a community or spiritual family and to persevere in it by loving each other the way we need to. We have lost a lot of power in the church today because we are not struggling to live in unity within a community and have in many cases accepted the easy individualism that marks many of the industrialized nations of the North. The focus on the common good, interdependence, and community life through the extended family that can still be found in many nations of the South has much to offer the world church. It is important that this gift not be lost because churches in all nations are facing the threat of accommodating to cultural norms and losing their witness as salt, light, and yeast. The obvious power of the community described in Acts was its clear allegiance to God's order no matter what sacrifice that belief and lifestyle required.

### The Community of Communities

As we consider how we could build healing communities within our own context, it may be helpful to look at examples of those who have tried to incorporate many basic tenets of the early church into their life together.

One such example can be found in a diverse group of communities in North America that formed a network of fellowship called the Community of Communities in 1975. For the next several years, this network held annual meetings, leadership conferences, inter-community visitations, and regional gatherings to explore issues of common concern and offering pastoral support to one another. They shared a vision of rebuilding the church by calling it to be a witness to the gospel and an agent of change in the world.

The network represented an ecumenical participation of traditions and races including various Protestant denominations as well as Roman Catholic, evangelical, and Anabaptist communities. The communities represented local church fellowships both within and outside denominational structures. They were located in urban and rural environments and in various racial or ethnic communities, including black, Hispanic, white, and racially mixed neighborhoods.

An excerpt from the Community of Communities statement explained their purpose:

> People from divergent traditions and histories are coming together in a movement of biblical faith and Christian conscience, offering a message of hope. Drawn together by the Spirit and the historical crisis we confront, we believe that the unity we have come to share is the work of the God of history, who has knit us together in love, fellowship, and a common vision of the gospel.
>
> The old divisions are beginning to break down — divisions between spirituality and politics, pastoral and prophetic ministry, worship and action, prayer and peace-making, evangelism and social action, biblical study and political analysis. In more and more places, the voice of the church is being raised in a cry for justice and peace.

The political and economic establishments can no longer count on the silence of the church when their policies crush the poor, deny human rights, and threaten nuclear holocaust.

The Community of Communities is part of a growing fellowship of people who seek to embody in their lives the changes and commitments the gospel calls for in our historical situation. Our commitments are simple: to deepen our discipleship to Jesus Christ; to study the Bible and pray together; to live simply, serve the poor, and make peace; to build community, to seek ever deeper conversion in our own lives; and to proclaim the good news of the gospel in the world.[28]

One has only to reflect on these goals to see the similarity with the ecclesial base communities of Latin America, Asia, and Africa. Surely in this manifesto there is a common theme shared by many in the world church. For there can be no healing community without a commitment to justice.

For the larger church, the challenge is to recognize how we are each being asked in our own context with our various traditions to embody the radical nonconforming message of the church described in Acts and the epistles.

# 4. You Have Been Christ to Me

## The Story of Community Covenant Church

Beloved let me be your servant,
let me be as Christ to you;
pray that I may have the grace
to let you be my servant, too.

We are pilgrims on a journey,
we are family on the road;
we are here to help each other
walk the mile and bear the load.

I will hold the Christ-light for you
in the night time of your fear;
I will hold my hand out to you,
speak the peace you long to hear.

I will weep when you are weeping;
when you laugh I'll laugh with you.
I will share your joy and sorrow
'til we've seen this journey through.

— The Servant Song[29]

The radical example of the early church has been the inspiration for Christian churches everywhere. How they incorporate the message is widely varied, but I believe it may be useful to describe the community that shaped my life for ten years. For it is here, more than anywhere else, that I have personally understood what it means to work at building healing community.

Community Covenant Church of Missoula, Montana, was established as a Swedish Mission Church in 1893, and it remained Swedish in language, culture, and doctrine until the 1920s. Eventually, the denomination became known as the Evangelical Covenant Church of North America. Although the church has maintained ties with the denomination for almost one hundred years, it underwent a major reconfiguration during the 1960s and 1970s that make it almost unrecognizable today as the ethnic Swedish congregation it once was. The congregational renewal during the late 1960s shaped the community as it exists today. And that renewal transformed an ordinary struggling congregation into a healing community that has been ministering to people in body, mind, and spirit during the past twenty-five years, despite conflict and change.

The transformation from church to healing community took place under the leadership of a pastor named Dan Simmons, who arrived in Missoula when the church had been undergoing a rapid succession of pastors and was dying. Dan came out of a Pentecostal church background and had a high level of interest in the charismatic renewal that was sweeping North America in the late 1960s and early 1970s. He immediately shared his vision of the church as a community bound together by the disciplines of the early church with the people he had come to pastor. He then began to hold regular meetings in addition to Sunday worship in which he encouraged the congregation to commit themselves to this kind of corporate life. Tension with the older members of the congregation surfaced, and there were attempts to eliminate Dan. But news of the new life that people were experiencing in the church was spreading throughout the town. Young people from the nearby university as well as people from the Jesus movement arrived at its doorstep.

Many of these young people were casualties of the hippy drug culture and had a very urgent need for healing, including drug detoxification, freedom from the wounds of sexual promiscuity, and mending shattered idealism. Some suffered from serious mental imbalance. All who came were welcomed and received into the community with open arms. During those years Dan's home became a sanctuary for many troubled people in search of healing. It was not unusual for one of Dan's four children to stumble over someone sleeping on the floor if they awoke in the night. These events took place during the height of the renewal movement in North America, and what was happening to Community Covenant Church was happening all over the country.

As in many traditional churches undergoing renewal, there was a split between the old members and the new community that was being born. Eventually only ten members of the 1968 congregation remained. The new congregation was composed of college students, counter-culture people, and working people. The community began meeting daily for prayer, Bible study, and teaching, and members' lives were changed dramatically.

Dan believed that people could be healed of any affliction through prayer. Consequently the new church spent a great deal of time in prayer with one another. The expression of the charismatic gifts, including speaking in tongues, prophecy, exhortation, and even the casting out of evil spirits practiced by Jesus and the disciples, were part of community life. All these New Testament gifts were introduced to the community through teaching, and Dan challenged the church to accept them as part of ordinary community life. The use of charismatic gifts to promote healing and wholeness within the community created a sense of immediacy that was very compelling. Things were happening in this place! The mainstream churches from which many members of the community came, in contrast, seemed to have lost their power to transform either lives or larger society.

As the community grew, new leaders were identified to share pastoral responsibility with Dan. Small fellowship groups called Acts Households were established, and these groups met weekly for prayer, Bible study, and mutual support. The groups were facilitated by leaders called household pastors, who were designated by the pastoral team. Together the pastoral team, household pastors, and members of a diaconate formed the governing body of Community Covenant Church.

### Community Covenant's Ministries

At the height of the renewal the church had 150 members. Today it has less. But during the years from 1968 to 1991 the church gave birth to over fifteen ministries. The ministries began with a series of coffee houses and grew to include a pre-school and elementary school, a rural retreat center, a print shop, residential homes for the developmentally disabled, a job cooperative, a table-making business, a rural drug rehabilitation center, an environmental institute and pastoral counseling center, a restaurant, and a natural food store. Community Covenant Church is a good example of the ministry and presence in the broader community produced by a small group of people that was typical of the highly committed communities of the 1960s and 1970s.

Emmaus Road Restaurant was the first official ministry of the church. The rationale for this ministry was expressed by a longtime member in a question and answer: "Why did the church get into the restaurant business? Very literally to feed the Lord's lambs." Many who came to the church were homeless and jobless, or had marginal employment no longer appropriate to their new lifestyle, such as selling drugs. The church leadership saw a need to create jobs within the community that could sustain these people and help them to grow in their new life together. This resulted in the church establishing a non-profit corporation called Anchor Fellowship with four tenets:

- To provide work for those community members who needed it.

- To be a medium of discipleship for those workers.

- To be a place of hospitality based on the belief that each customer, like Jesus, was to be served lovingly.

- To use any income above operating costs for mission.

Emmaus Road Restaurant developed a large following in the town and provided economic support for many in the church. The restaurant ministry was also successful in supporting many other local ministries as well as World Relief.

This was also true of the Good Food Store, a natural food store that came into the hands of the church after two of its owners became Christians. Both of these ministries provided not only jobs for members of the church, but opportunities to serve the larger city. Customers were often attracted to the church by the quality of life they sensed when receiving services from either enterprise.

Another area of ministry the church chose to pursue was group homes for disabled men and women. These homes were modeled after the L'Arche communities of Canadian Jean Vanier, which attempt to build communities based on mutual love and respect between the disabled and those called to staff the homes. Although there has been changeover of staff during the past fifteen years, the residents are the same men and women for whom the homes came into existence. The men and women who live in these homes have become members of the worshipping community of the church and their presence has shaped the worship experience in a unique way. Relationships with these brothers and sisters have given the community a sensitivity toward special needs of the disabled and enriched the community's life. From the earlier experiences with members who were casualties of the drug experiments of the 1960s, the community has learned to recognize brokenness in those who are not outwardly disabled, but who carry an equally deep need to be made whole.

New Creation Institute, which focused on healing the environment and the person, took its inspiration from the passage in 2 Corinthians that says that if anyone is in Christ there is a whole new world. We felt this ministry expressed the biblical *shalom* that we were experiencing in our community life as well as important service to the larger community and church. The counseling center has expanded and is providing much needed service to low-income people who are seeking help from people with a spiritual commitment.

Community Covenant's many and varied ministries through the years have always expressed both the inward and the outward journey necessary for Christians responding to human need. Prophetic engagement in the world political scene has accompanied the more pastoral ministries of counseling, evangelism, and healing the sick. Members have participated in protest at state and regional military bases that produce nuclear weapons. Some have traveled to Latin America as members of Witness for Peace. Still others have become involved in the Middle East conflict and participated in peace camps there. There has been a long tradition of making a public peace witness on Good Friday. During the recent war in the Gulf, members of the church assembled daily in prayer and protest at the city hall with other townspeople. These ministries and protests are all examples of ways the church has sought to witness to the power of the cross over all forms of death and to go beyond itself to minister to the cries of a needy world.

Much of the transformation of people's lives that has taken place in the church since its renewal has been due to a sense of being called to provide shelter for those in need. This special gift more than anything else has united the community in a common purpose through the years. The shelter provided to people has been literal, but also a haven of emotional and psychological safety. Poet Robert Frost called this kind of shelter home: "Home is the place where when you go there, they have to take you in." That form of unconditional hospitality has set this church apart for many years. Although there have been significant changes and many areas of witness during the past twenty-five years, the church always returns to this first sense of calling that embodies its understanding of the gospel mandate.

Another unifying principle of the community's life has been the earnest desire both to be made whole and to participate in restoring God's *shalom* to the whole earth. Most of the people who later became members initially gravitated to the church because they sensed that it was a place where healing was taking place. This emphasis on healing and wholeness was introduced by Dan Simmons, but it quickly became a rallying point for the whole church. Community Covenant eagerly accepted the charge to become a healing community. This transformation was accomplished in part by incorporating prayer for healing into daily life. Interceding for and with one another about all manner of concerns from the personal to the political was the daily bread of life together.

Intercession took place within the weekly Acts Households, in corporate worship, and in special weeks of prayer in which the whole community was gathered. The whole range of charismatic gifts was used in prayer for healing of body, mind, or spirit. Early on the community established a prayer chapel in the sanctuary of the church. In its weekly celebration of the Eucharist, an invitation is still given that anyone in need of healing in body, mind, or spirit is welcomed to the prayer room where someone is waiting to pray with them. This prayer for healing includes the rite of anointment with oil following the account in James 5, where the community is encouraged to go to the elders of the community for prayer and anointment with oil. The ministry of prayer for healing is shared among pastors, members of the community who have been identified as those with gifts in healing, and members of the Acts Households.

Through the years there have been many testimonies to the various kinds of healing that have taken place as a result of the prayers that were offered in the prayer room and in other places. Some of these healings have been from physical illness. Others have involved healing in broken relationships, and still others have concerned the healing of emotional and psychological illness. There have also been many instances when the desired healing cannot be seen. But the practice of prayer for healing has always stimulated a release of spiritual power that is nourishing to the whole community.

The church quickly learned that there are no magic formulas where prayer is concerned. Many who received prayer did not receive the healing they hoped for. A young father died of cancer in our midst after months of almost constant prayer and aggressive medical treatment, and a healthy woman delivered stillborn twins. Yet it became clear that to pray for healing is a way of living in hopeful expectation that God is present and active in our lives. This assumption and being in dialogue with God are healing. Whether or not people were cured as a result of our prayers, we saw that God was always drawing us into wholeness and challenging us to deeper faith.

### Conflict and Change

After seventeen years of building healing community in Missoula, this fertile season of community life came to an abrupt end when our founding pastor accepted a new call to ministry in the Middle East. The changes that have taken place since then have severely tested the community's powers of recuperation and ability to maintain its healing mission.

It was only in the face of Dan Simmons's departure that the community saw how he had been the glue that held all the various liberal and conservative groups together. The tensions that surfaced with force following his departure focused on biblical interpretations and the church's witness in the world. Members had reached different conclusions about our mission and purpose. We were no longer unified in a common vision. The role of women and our public peace witness had become particularly divisive. These are not unusual issues to be disputed within any church. But they divided our community in a rending way. The efforts to deal openly with the conflict through a council of reconciliation were only partially successful. Many people left the community disillusioned that neither our high level of commitment to each other nor our knowledge and experience with healing many kinds of wounds was great enough to keep the community intact.

This time of conflict and loss of members has caused Community Covenant Church to reexamine its mission and purpose. There is a new appreciation of the difficulty of achieving unity in the midst of an uneasy diversity of theology and personality types. The church is still recuperating from facing conflict and adapting to a new style of leadership based on consensus. Community life is no longer as clear and unequivocal as it was in the first blush of the renewal.

Why tell a story about a community that couldn't

manage to heal itself in a book on healing community? Because the whole church has a great deal to learn about the art of conflict resolution and genuine reconciliation. Healing communities are not utopian ideals. The experience of people with a passionate commitment to be instruments of healing in a broken world who failed to resolve their own internal conflict shows us that healing communities are also wounded communities. Catholic priest Henri Nouwen reminds us that good pastors are wounded healers. This is the paradox we live with, the mystery that we can't solve.

Christian theology and story remind us, however, that where there is death there is also new life to be found. The conflict that brings an end to one season of life may lead to new ways to go on together — how to reconcile at deeper levels and how to discover a new unifying mission and purpose. This, after all, is always the task for Christians.

Many of the healing communities I have known have experienced similar conflict and change. The intensity of the conflict is very painful because of the covenant relationships that are broken between some members. The words of Ecclesiastes that there is a time to be born and a time to die and a season for everything under the sun help to make sense of the breakdown of the old and the search for new life in community. Or in the words of Dr. David Hilton, it is not a sign of failure when a community dies any more than when a person dies. All they have learned from the struggle with what it means to love one another as God has loved us speaks with integrity to us all. Christian community causes us to grow through the sometimes painful risks we take, but without these risks we cannot know the joy that comes uniquely in life together.

> When we sing to God in heaven
> we shall find such harmony,
> born of all we've known together
> of Christ's love and agony.
> — The Servant Song

# 5. Pressing On

## The Discipline of Life Together

> Come, let us return to the Lord;
> for it is he who has torn, and he will heal us;
> he has wounded us, and he will bind us up.
> After two days he will revive us; on the third
> day he will raise us up,
> that we may live before him.
>
> Let us press on to know the Lord;
> his appearing is as sure as the dawn;
> he will come to us like the showers,
> like the spring rains that water the earth.
>
> — Hosea 6:1–3

Anyone who has made a commitment in marriage or community life can easily recognize the role of discipline in life together. After the honeymoon is over, discipline plays an important role in helping us continue to keep our vows to another person or group. Some years ago, while I was a member of Community Covenant Church, our pastor preached a sermon on community life that I have always remembered. The essence was in its title: "I Press On." It was based on the text in the third chapter of Philippians that says,

> Not that I have already obtained this or have already reached the goal; but I press on to make it my own, because Christ Jesus has made me his own.... I do not consider that I have made it my own; but this one thing I do: forgetting what lies behind and straining forward to what lies ahead, I press on toward the goal for the prize of the heavenly call of God in Jesus Christ.

How often I have thought about those words and all they imply. One of the paradoxes I see in community life is that it depends on both grace and hard work. I don't think it is possible to experience community in the absence of either. And though there is clearly a sense in which community is a gift no matter how one strives, it is also true that in healing community persevering plays a major role. Or as my Swedish grandmother used to say, "Work and pray, but heavy on the work!"

Building healing community in our troubled world takes discipline. Everything we see in the culture mitigates against it. Particularly in the rich and powerful nations of the North, we live in cultures that promise instant reward and gratification of all our needs. In contrast, the healing communities I have known are all based on covenant living. In some cases the covenant may be implicit rather than written and signed. But more often covenants have been formal and entered into only after an extended period of study and reflection.

There are many examples of covenant statements. The one used in Community Covenant Church in Montana contained these words:

> By God's grace I covenant to follow Jesus Christ, my Lord and Saviour, in common with this community, to submit myself to my brothers and sisters in the fear and love of Christ; to live, serve, and celebrate the Kingdom of God with these people until the Lord consummates time for me, or calls me to life and service in another part of the Body of Christ.[30]

Another example is this covenant from the Church of the Saviour in Washington, D.C.:

*The Commitment:*

> I come today to join a local expression of the Church, which is the body of those on whom the call of God rests to witness the grace and truth of God.
>
> I recognize that the function of the Church is to glorify God in adoration and sacrificial service, and to be God's missionary to the world, bearing witness to God's redeeming grace in Jesus Christ.
>
> I believe as did Peter that Jesus is the Christ, the Son of the Living God.
>
> I unreservedly and with abandon commit my life and destiny to Christ, promising to give Him a practical priority in all the affairs of life. I will seek first the Kingdom of God and His Righteousness.
>
> I commit myself, regardless of the expenditures of time, energy, and money, to becoming an informed, mature Christian.

I believe that God is the total owner of my life and resources. I give God the throne in relation to the material aspect of my life. God is the owner, I am the ower. Because God is a lavish giver I too shall be lavish and cheerful in my regular gifts.

Realizing that Jesus taught and exemplified a life of love, I will seek to be loving in all relations with individuals, groups, classes, races, and nations and will seek to be a reconciler, living in a manner which will end all war, personal and public.

I will seek to bring every phase of my life under the lordship of Christ.

When I move from this place I will join some other expression of the Christian Church.[31]

The covenants in the Old Testament were always marked by a sign such as circumcision or sacrifices. In the New Testament baptism and communion as sacraments are called an outward sign of an inward grace — baptism marking entrance into the community and communion as continued fellowship with Christ and his Body. Covenanting is made public so that we as God's people will remember who we are. The context for all such covenanting is God's covenant with us.

### Keeping the Covenant

It is easy to see that covenants like these are not something into which a person enters lightly. In many cases a person may undergo a year or even more of preparation for membership. Some communities identify these periods of reflection and preparation for making a membership commitment as novitiates, such as one finds in the Roman Catholic tradition. Novitiates are a time of getting acquainted with the history of a community and with its vision, common beliefs, or creeds. It is a period in which people are asked to consider seriously whether God has called them to this community in this part of the world for this season of their life. During this time of internship, novices are usually guided by older members of the community who can help them determine whether this will be the right community for them and also to respond to questions that arise along the way.

My own understanding of the need for a formal covenant is that it is a call or invitation to deeper experiences of community life that become more real as we submit to the everyday discipline of sharing our life decisions, our time, our money, and our feelings. The main purpose of any such covenant is to hold ourselves and each other accountable to these freeing, chosen actions that can guide us into deeper fellowship or communion with Christ and each other. Our focus through the covenant is to follow Christ's call to form a new family based on love, worship, service, and a desire to discern and follow God's will individually and corporately.

In my own life in community, it became necessary to ask for help in keeping the covenant many times. In particular, we turned to others during a time when my husband and I were receiving frequent invitations to travel and speak to other churches and groups. This was when our children were very young and we were each carrying several part-time jobs, including participation in the pastoral team of the church, to support ourselves economically. These invitations and the travel they involved became an occasion for much tension between us. I did not relish staying home with the children any more than my husband did. We both wanted to be able to respond to these opportunities for contact throughout the world church. Yet we knew that our family needed stability and the presence of at least one of us most of the time. Repeated separation was difficult.

When we fell into the traditional pattern of our culture, that the woman stays home to feather the nest while the man goes out in search of food and adventure, our marriage became strained. We felt unable to continue in this repeated decision-making crisis. At this point we enlisted the help of some trusted friends in the community to meet with us and help us sift through the invitations together. We even gave the process a name. We called it the travel discernment group, which is exactly how it functioned.

We had invited people we felt saw the whole picture and were able to be advocates for each of us plus the children and the marriage. We believed that they probably had a larger understanding of God's purposes for us than we did ourselves during that stressful time. Having called this group together on our own behalf, we felt bound to listen carefully to them and to take their counsel after we had each made our cases.

It was a wonderfully liberating experience to share the burden of making all these choices in isolation — an isolation that causes many marriages to shatter. This is only one example of what covenant living can offer anyone who wants to submit to the love and judgment of others in the interest of being a more faithful and integrated person.

But it is only natural in the midst of discipline and hard work to rebel and look for an easier way to live our lives. Committing oneself to one other person is difficult enough, but covenanting to a whole group of people with whom we may have little in common but our spiritual quest can break down in a moment. This is why many communities renew their commitment or vows on a yearly basis. It seems crucial that any covenant must be based on an act of free will if it is to endure. In the act of harnessing one's will and remaining obedient or faithful to what one believes one has been called to, there can be freedom and a renewed sense of purpose.

I reached such a crossroad in 1986 during the period of multiple jobs, travel, and young children. During that year I saw clearly that my relationship with the Lord was a reflection of my relationship to the church community. So that when things were proceeding harmoniously in community life as they were during the first five years of our life together, I had a deep sense of joy and purpose and I felt a close connection to God's love and call on my life. When, in contrast, my own life was fragmented and the community was threatening to splinter over issues of women in leadership and peace witness, I felt nothing but despair at the seeming absence of God. So when the question of renewing the covenant came up for me that year, I faced a dilemma. I felt like quitting, dropping out of community life — and surely I did withdraw during that period. But faced with the reminder and the seriousness of the commitment I had made in the past, I felt, as I did in my marriage, that I must renew out of obedience and hope that what was damaged could be restored.

We were all asked to write a reflection as part of the process of renewing the membership commitment. In mine I told the community of my struggle, my disillusionment, and my anger. I also told them of my intention to press ahead in the hope of a resurrection of my feelings of being unified in purpose together. I believed that in the act of persevering, void of good feelings, there was the possibility of crossing over and experiencing new life in my feelings about the community and in my relationship to God.

By God's grace two opportunities to gain perspective in the midst of this struggle emerged. One was attending a gathering of women in ministry with a woman from our pastoral team and being encouraged and blessed for the struggle we were engaged in at home in our efforts to pastor those who didn't want to be pastored by women. The second opportunity came while I was teaching a seminary course on the healing ministry of the church in which we gave some time to prayer for healing with one another. As we formed a circle and each in turned received prayer with the laying on of hands and anointment of oil, I received from my students a powerful reminder of my own need to be healed. In spite of my own efforts to remain distant and academic about the subject, I was reached by the manifestation of God's presence through the hands of my brothers and sisters — students not well known to me or to each other, who simply opened themselves to this opportunity for healing. It was a turning point in my life within my own community. I returned to the community ready to renew the covenant without asking that all the conflicts be resolved.

Perhaps as importantly, I recognized my own need to be healed from the tyranny of emotion as some rejected and others accepted me. This recognition reminded me of the need for a relationship with God that was rooted in something more enduring than human approval. I have a strong sense that this kind of rootedness is a core issue for many people.

One of the learnings out of this time of struggle to reaffirm the covenant relationship to the community was to see that community life, like marriage, has dry seasons. Another learning was that communities are as wounded as the people who compose them. Thus we should not be surprised when trouble surfaces. Achieving unity of purpose in the presence of diverse personalities is hard work. Pressing on means that one must learn through an act of discipline to embrace the community in its many faces — to belong to one another more deeply in spite of our amazingly diverse ways.

### A Variety of Disciplines

Because covenanting within a healing community requires such a high degree of commitment, most communities find that there is a need for a group of disciplines that help the covenanter keep her or his focus. For one can easily see that the covenants included here are not covenants to a detailed set of doctrinal positions or to a constitution and by-laws. Rather, they are covenants of grace, discipleship, fellowship, service, and celebration. In them one finds the clear desire to become the body of Christ or family of faith in a real place with real people and even in the face of real conflicts. So keeping the covenant necessarily involves finding a way through difficult relationships and the very real issues that divide people the world over.

If we believe, however, that the main purpose of the church is to embody God's life in the world through the word, grace, spirit, and the gifts we have been given, that process may be assisted by the age-old spiritual disciplines. Someone has said that disciplines of Christian life are useful to prepare the soil of our lives to receive the breadth of the spirit of Christ within. They cannot be used as a basis on which to justify ourselves and prove our goodness. If that were the aim, most would fail the test.

During the year I spent as part of the Church of the Saviour, I was unable to get over the hurdle of their accepted disciplines, which included fifty minutes daily in prayer, Scripture reading, meditation, and the keeping of a spiritual journal. Because of this inability to see the disciplines as a means of grace and greater freedom in my own life, I remained an intern member. But I had a wise and gifted spiritual director who stayed close beside me during that period of self-doubt and enabled me to see that the keeping of spiritual disciplines does not make us worthy. Rather, as in any endeavor worth doing, regular disciplines provide us with a useful structure that others before us have tested and found valuable. And in the repetition of these acts, many discover a freedom and a clarity of purpose for their lives that they have never known before. It may also need to be said that different disciplines fit with certain temperaments better than others, so communities need to provide as many ways as possible to help people find the discipline that best suits them.

Another example from my early life in community may be helpful. I had just returned from two years in another country when I married. I moved to the town where my husband had been established for several years and joined his church and community. Much to my dismay, his small mission group within the church had decided to accept a discipline of silent meditation during their one hour meeting before waiting tables for the night at the church's coffee house. They all had demanding jobs and found deep inner refreshment through this corporate act of worship.

But for me it was miserable. I was alone all day and making a number of demanding transitions like marriage, returning from another culture, and forming a new set of significant relationships. I came to dread those Thursday nights at the Potter's House and wouldn't have made it successfully through the experience without the wise counsel of the pastor, Gordon Cosby, who gently suggested that what is liberating for one may be poison to another. He asked if I would consider looking for a mission group that better fit my own needs. That was a liberating word that freed me to discover my own path for drawing close to God and to service through the church. One could wish that we were each wise enough to allow that there are many ways to move toward God. Our real task as Christians is to help one another to press toward God and toward discovering the work God has given us to do.

Just as each community may use its own formal or informal membership commitment, so it is that communities have many forms of discipline. But if they are examined closely one will find much common ground. An outline of commonly accepted disciplines found in many types of healing communities would certainly include:

- *Prayer:* A daily time of individual or private prayer, corporate prayer times at home, and participation in community events such as retreats and special worship focused on corporate prayer.

- *Worship:* Preparation for and participation in the regular worship life of the community.

- *Fellowship:* A life that is open, shared, and given to others in a concrete context such as a regular small group.

- *Study:* A commitment to spending regular time with reading and reflection on the Bible, both individually and in group study on issues that concern everyone.

- *Gifts/Servanthood:* A process of discovering, having confirmed, and offering one's unique gifts for the benefit of the community.

- *Lifestyle:* Sharing resources, regular giving through tithe or other means, and an effort to simplify one's life as a response to the needs of others and to the abundance of gifts God provides.

- *Mission/Witness:* Finding a way to live the gospel in an open declaration of the centrality of God in our lives. Responding concretely to the words of the prophet Micah who told us that God requires us to do justice, love mercy, and walk humbly with God.[32]

No one and no community can live out all the disciplines of Christian life at the same time. Some communities place more emphasis on justice than mercy, but the integrated and truly healing community will embrace a variety of disciplines that call people to mature and draw closer to God. Ruth and Loren Halvorsen, founders of the Arc Community in Minnesota, have identified action, reflection, and celebration as keynotes of community life. After fifteen years of building a retreat ministry in the woods of Minnesota with various kinds of people, they believe that community life must offer worship, work, study, and celebration if it is to be healing to people and nations.

What enables people and communities to commit themselves in an ongoing way to spiritual disciplines and covenant living? What explains the motivation for this committed way of living? The explanation is that Christian community is life-giving. The findings of the Christian Medical Commission in their study on health, healing, and wholeness suggest that it is the sense of belonging and purpose that comes in part from a discovery of our own gifts and how we are to offer them to the larger community that is profoundly empowering.

# 6. The Death of the Dream

## Conflict in Community Life

> When C. S. Lewis was bottoming out as an atheist in 1929, but before he bottomed up as a Christian, he looked inside himself and saw "a zoo of lusts, a bedlam of ambitions, a nursery of fears, a harem of fondled hatreds." This is the point that all saints reach when they confront their inner selves.
>
> — William Griffin

While it may be inspiring to think of creating heaven on earth, as one author has referred to communal ventures, actually living with other people and submitting all that is important to us to their discernment can be closer to hell. Or, as another author on community has said, "Whenever two or three are gathered together, even in His name, there will be tension."[33]

We can never underestimate the brokenness that exists in us all. That people can come together and be unified around a common vision even for a while is a triumph of Christ's resurrecting power. Communities are not utopia, although that is what motivates many who seek them out. Thus when conflict emerges and the dream dissolves, many leave. For this reason, the dream of living happily ever after in community must be replaced by a theology of the cross — an understanding that prepares the person and the community for pain and conflict, disillusionment, and change, and for new life out of death.

If communities are not providing a way of understanding the life and death cycles that affect all groups, they are missing an important task. A community that isn't prepared for conflict may be deeply wounded rather than healed by the experience of life together.

Communities are full of pain and conflict because people's lives are marked with struggle. A pastor, reflecting on the level of pain present in his community, addressed the question of healing:

> One thing I observe is how much people in the community are hurting — long-time, faithful participants in our common life suffering from depression, results of broken relationships, wrestling with sin in their lives, and yet

persevering, pressing on. This is something of a curiosity, since we have given so much attention to healing and the wholeness of Christ in our lives over the past years. Perhaps this is the experience of the "wounded healer" as Henri Nouwen describes it — God's way of helping us to stay in touch with the suffering of the world, and enlarging our hearts to care for those God brings our way.

But I can't help wondering if this is not a season for healing, if this year isn't a time where we again do caring for those hurting among us. Could this not be a year of relief, freedom, and health for places of chronic suffering?

... I have great anticipation for the healing that I know God wants to do among us. But there is also great potential for factions and division. But that is the tension that we've always lived with. It's the thing that keeps us so dependent on the grace of God, the mercy of our Lord Jesus, and the guidance of the Holy Spirit. It is simply impossible to fit ourselves together by ourselves and to fit the ministries that God has called us to into place without God's help.[34]

The subject of conflict in community life can be approached by looking at some of the psychological factors that come into play. First, we must remember that any attempt to form community with people who were previously strangers is an unnatural act that goes against the training that many have received about not mixing outside the family. In community, not only are we in close contact with strangers, but we are in the process of creating a new family with these people. The creation of a new family in Christ is a radical act in any society because it demands that we travel outside the accepted boundaries of our culture to embrace the stranger and live in intimacy together. One can even speak of the necessity of being converted into community life, because it involves choosing to live by different rules. Forming community means turning around and making a break with one's former life — like scriptural *metanoia*. All the normal categories change.

At the same time, there is a way in which living with other people in an attempt to be a family recreates many of the dynamics we have experienced in our original family experience. Since there is no one who can claim to have had a perfect childhood, the old wounds will inevitably surface in a new attempt to live intimately with strangers. Whatever we have carried with us into adulthood of trust or mistrust, acceptance or rejection, independence or dependence, competition or cooperation is often relived in the context of the new family with whom we have chosen to share our lives and goals.

An example of this kind of reliving of one's early family experience in a new setting is often reflected in the relationship to those in authority. Leaders in the community frequently receive projections from people who have not resolved their feelings about their relationships with their father or mother and others in authority. When the community leader asks them to accept certain conditions or stipulations about community life, they often rebel in ways strongly reminiscent of earlier adolescence. Sibling rivalry is an even more acute struggle for some people, as they form a strong attachment to the often charismatic leader and feel threatened when their affection is not returned, or when others receive more acknowledgment or position in the community's life.

The success of a healing community, in fact, depends more on flexibility than on inspiration, because when we enter community life we need an attitude of complete openness to the experience and actions of others. Forming community involves abandoning our isolated individualism and joining with others in a sense of common purpose and common activities aimed at achieving those new goals. There are many psychological dropouts from community life because of this demanding process. A successful community experience depends on many things, including a sense of reciprocity between the individual and the community. As Jean Vanier has described it, in his book *Community and Growth*, the individual must eventually make a transition from "the community for me — to, me for the community." Community fails where people fail to make this transition. Insurmountable obstacles, such as the woundedness we have been describing, prevent them from learning to take satisfaction in giving themselves to the pursuit of a common life. This is a complex issue because individuals are being challenged to give themselves to the community and its ideals while at the same time to preserve a sense of self. The ability to do both depends on a sense of separateness. Healthy communities depend on a balance between individual and corporate life. If persons are not secure in their identity, they may be unable to distinguish between community goals and personal goals or between advice from the leadership and their own need to direct their life choices.

People often seek out community life because of a great need to be loved, accepted, and healed, but they have very little to give in return. The community may be so absorbed in its mission that it ignores the emotional needs of its members. This can create a tragic mismatch. If the focus on the common good is so exclusive that there is little pastoral care, an individual may have to leave the community to preserve health and growth. People also leave because they lack the ability to meet the demands of communal interaction, they cannot respond creatively to the disciplines and authority, or they become psychologically exhausted by the effort to live in unity with others. Integrating the needs of individual members and being effective in mission beyond the community are the challenges faced by all communities.

It is simply the case that healing communities do not bring healing to everyone who comes to share in their life. For those who see community life as a panacea to problems they have previously been unable to manage, the outlook is not good. What most communities can realistically offer those in search of healing is a sense of purpose for their lives, which in many but certainly not all cases will be an effective cure. But it is essential that individuals approach community life with a deep sense of participation in its corporate vision rather than an overwhelming need for healing, or there is bound to be frustration on all sides.

### Wounding Communities

It is not only the handicaps of individuals that prevent a healing experience in community from taking place, however. The heart of the community itself may be unhealthy or deficient in some important way. In some communities, for example, there is a focus on psychological comfort that requires the avoidance of conflict at all costs. Communities who cannot survive tension become very dysfunctional just as families do. Communities with no internal cohesiveness will not succeed either. A community needs a strong sense of its identity and mission. But there must be a balance, because there is also a danger of a community becoming too authoritarian, and this is a realistic threat to individuals who lack the strength of conviction to defend their own experience.

Finally, some communities encourage an unhealthy dependence in their members, and this discourages people from being accountable for their own life before God in a way that keeps them empowered. The kind of ongoing vulnerability required is very demanding and requires preparation. Healing communities could benefit from the novice experience required in the Roman Catholic tradition before one makes a final commitment to community life, because living intimately with other people to achieve a common purpose does not come automatically in many cultures.

Despite all its rich potential, community can be wounding. A disappointing reality of community life is that sharing a common vision does not protect people from intense likes and dislikes. Feelings of insecurity, jealousy, distrust, or desire for control inevitably surface, and they have a devastating impact within all communities.

Community conflict occurs at three levels. The first is interpersonal, including differences in personality and lifestyle that reveal themselves in preferences about modern or traditional music in worship, debates about individual versus common cup in communion, and dozens of other matters.

The second level focuses on theological differences. Common examples of theological conflict are the issues of divorce and remarriage, the role of women in leadership in the church, adult versus infant baptism, adherence to creeds, and views of the priesthood.

The final layer of conflict revolves around the community vision or purpose. Most communities coalesce around a clear vision aimed either at the person or at institutions. This can be described as the pastoral or the prophetic witness of the church. Communities dedicated to bringing justice to the poor and to those oppressed by unresponsive institutions are sometimes thought of as justice communities that are responding to the prophetic and liberating message of the Scriptures. They spend the greatest portion of their mission energy on acts of social justice that can be anything from working to provide fair and affordable housing to acts of civil disobedience in response to the build-up of nuclear weapons or the imprisonment of innocent people. The pastoral communities are focused on the inward life of a person — on spiritual, psychological, emotional, and physical needs for healing.

Entire communities have divided over the question of which is the most valid form of obedience to the biblical mandate to go into all the world and make disciples of all nations. That is why Graham Pulkingham, an Episcopalian rector who established renewed communities in his Texas parish and in England and Scotland, once said that there needed to be as many different kinds of communities as there are people. No community can be or do everything, even those that try to embrace and integrate both the pastoral and prophetic dimensions of ministry. Perhaps placing a stronger value on the diverse personal and theological interpretations present in the Body of Christ that is the church worldwide would enable people to create many different kinds of communities, and this might release some of the expectations of what one community in one context can do.

By making a serious attempt to find unity amid the diversity of personality, lifestyle, theological orientation, and vision of what is needed to create a just society, communities are attempting what most would immediately consider impossible. It is no wonder, then, that these multiple levels of conflict disrupt and at times destroy community life. Anyone studying communities must reckon with these forces of tension. And anyone actually engaged in community life must find the way through as well as how to recover from conflict. It has already been said that Christians are inadequately prepared to deal creatively with conflict. We have no training, and this is very evident in the number of divorces and casualties between parents and children. This handicap is present in family life and is all the more present in a group that is not bound by blood but by ideas about spiritual truth.

### Facing Failure

But what can the church look to that would lead people through these multiple layers of conflict and into the deeper levels of acceptance or trust that enable community?

Whatever can help persons see their own need to repent for their uncharitable action and to be generous with forgiveness will offer a way through. There are stages in repentance that can lead to forgiveness. Something must happen that allows us to see our wrongness and to see the cost of it in our relationships. In genuine repentance we become eager to amend our own lives rather than to engage in judging the rightness or wrongness of another person. Some communities try to follow the scriptural injunction of urging members to address conflicts directly by going to the person involved and trying to find a peaceable solution together. It is very helpful if the persons involved in the conflict have not lost sight of their role in it.

In cases where communication is no longer possible, the leadership of the community can be helpful. The presence of a third party who is committed to both people to listen and offer counsel can help provide a solution. In such cases everyone benefits. But it would be dishonest to say that this approach is foolproof. There simply are too many things that can and do go wrong in the attempt to make peace, as is so apparent in the global community. All communities face power struggles and divisions over theological issues that erode their unity. Some of the conflicts prove to be irreconcilable despite everyone's best efforts.

In the church in Montana, an experienced community leader was asked to assist us after we met for three months to try to reach a compromise and to restore trust. We did written assignments that we shared in small groups and no dimension of the issues was left unspoken. Still we couldn't break the impasse any more than many married couples can. It seemed that the breakdown of trust and the conflict had been festering too long. We had tried to function by suppressing deeply felt but unresolved rifts in the interest of unity. There was no way to move forward together.

The Roman Catholic sister who came to meet with us toward the end of our own attempt at reconciliation offered a startling observation: Our community as we had known it was dying. We would either discover a new vision or go out of existence. The differences were irreconcilable and there seemed nothing left to do but let go. This observation led to a deep sense of mourning but we were not left without hope. We were given a larger framework in which we could see that communities have seasons to be born, to thrive, to dwindle, and to die — also to be reborn. It became a time to wait for the new.

What we are describing outlines common problems and even the breakdown of community life. For many people there is also a way that experiencing the new family in community can function as a concrete channel of God's grace and healing. Discovering who we are called by God to be can be one of the most creative ventures available. It is stimulating to experience the kind of self-knowledge that comes from communal interaction. By their responses, people offer you a mirror to see parts of yourself you would otherwise never discover. We do not always like what we see, but if love and forgiveness are present there is an opportunity to be healed that seldom arises for those who never let themselves be vulnerable in this way.

When we see ourselves as we really are the picture is not attractive. This is where the community can play a major role in mediating God's healing power. Most of us are alienated from God and God's purposes for us, like the prodigal son in the Scriptures. We need to be rescued by the love and forgiveness of God, and that acceptance can be mediated in a powerful way when a brother or sister in the community accepts us in a way that we have never accepted ourselves. Becoming a new person in Christ is a life-long process, but many of us flee from those parts of ourselves that we cannot manage. Instead we could seek companionship for our journey and gain the encouragement we need to make this pilgrimage toward being made whole.

The coming together in Christian community provides a place where we can be known. Here we can be known for who we really are, not the person we pretend to be or the person someone else thinks we ought to be. And here is the place to receive the liberating touch of Christ in our midst as we worship and serve along with others.

# 7. Faith to Go Out with Good Courage

## Seasons of Community Life

O Lord God, who has called us your servants to ventures of which we cannot see the ending, by paths as yet untrodden and through perils unknown: give us faith to go out with good courage, not knowing where we go, but only that your hand is leading us and your love supporting us; through Jesus Christ, our Lord. Amen.

— Holden Village Community
Lake Chelan, Washington

The intention in the early days of the renewal communities was to spend the rest of one's adult life together building community. In that goal there is a poignant echo of Christian marriage vows to do the same. Only a few communities that I know are still fulfilling that expectation, but the fact that even a few are remaining in one place with some of the same people over the long term is unique and worthy of notice in this highly mobile world. The Church of the Saviour, established in 1947, one year earlier than the World Council of Churches, was the first ecumenical church in Washington, D.C., and will soon be celebrating forty-five years in community.

For most communities, however, time has changed the expectation of permanence. People have come and gone. There are many reasons for this flux in membership. Some are based on people's inabilities to adhere to the commitments made by various covenant communities. Other reasons have to do with personal growth and changes in marital and family status. Single people may have more long-term success in community than families raising children, the most common reason being that families are communities in themselves. They also require commitment and major energy, so the family system and the community compete for limited resources and too many needs. It also happens that one partner of a marriage does not share the community vision of the other partner. When a permanent impasse is reached, these families leave the community.

Given the seriousness and zeal with which most people enter community life and pursue their mission, the death of a community is a grave experience. A community dissolves for many reasons, most quite readily apparent, but nonetheless painful. When a group in North America decided to end their life together after eight years, they shared six reasons that capture the essence of why communities sometimes fail. I include them here because I am confident that they are instructive to many who struggle to understand these painful endings:

1. Basic differences in vision and community structure. Lack of unanimity about pooling economic resources and the pace of communal life in relationship to earning a living and family needs.

2. Individual growth leading people to pursue their own interests away from the community.

3. Dwindling membership caused by exhaustion from ever expanding opportunities for ministry and human limitations of time and energy.

4. Loss of leadership caused by personal needs and differences in perspective on the community's life.

5. Personal trauma including loss of key community members, illness and death, and family crises involving both marriage partners and children.

6. The breakdown of trust between members resulting in strained relationships and interpersonal conflict.[35]

These six reasons are based on tensions that always exist in community life. In some cases they become the reasons a group cannot go on together. What is the pivotal ingredient that makes persevering through to resolution and new life impossible? Loss of trust in both the vision and the people seems to be the basis for the disintegration of community life. It is the erosion of trust that destroys the will to fight on and to continue to overcome differences and seek the common good. When a community dies, or a person withdraws from community life, something precious has been lost. The grief can be incapacitating and the damage to future visions irreparable. At the least, those ending their life together will be disoriented by this major loss and will have a season of extended mourning. What is being mourned? The death of a uniting vision of a new world rooted and grounded in God's love and justice and the loss of treasured companions on that journey. Nothing less than that.

Not all reasons for leaving communities are rooted in conflict. Sometimes people begin to sense an inner movement that alerts them to respond to God's mission elsewhere. They may be hearing words like these from Nietzsche: "Wake and listen.... From the future come winds with secret wing-beats; and good tidings are proclaimed to delicate ears.... Verily, the earth shall yet become a site of recovery and even now a new fragrance surrounds it, bringing salvation — and a new hope." Or from Jeremiah: "For surely I know the plans I have for you, says the Lord, plans for your welfare and not for harm, to give you a future with hope" (Jer. 29:11). Whatever they are hearing, something is stirring in their soul and change is in the wind.

## Stages of Development

There has also been a decisive shift away from the communal values that characterized North American values during the 1960s when many of these communities were born. Life in community is subject to change. It is often a process of asking what it means to be community here and now. Who are we becoming? What are our ministries to ourselves and in the larger world? Why are we involved in those particular places? What nurtures us individually and as a group? The answers to these and other questions usually contain the next steps on the journey for both individuals and the group. When these questions are raised, the responses may reflect some of these themes:

- We have changed.

- We have grown older and are no longer the same people we once were.

- Are we maturing or have we just grown old and less dedicated to the founding vision that drew us to community life?

- We want to reaffirm our basic structures and spiritual disciplines, but family life is competing with community gatherings.

- We are tired.

These responses illustrate that living in community is a dynamic, not static process. People need help to view these changes as something that can lead to new vision and purpose. Father Richard Rohr has identified primary seasons in community development.

The first stage is characterized by beginning euphoria, which includes feeling inspired and empowered. Community members are in love with the vision and the group. Most people want to stay in this stage forever because of what they are discovering about themselves and others in community life.

In stage two, people reluctantly fall out of love with the community and the people in it. They have discovered that the community and its leaders, theology, vision, and structures are imperfect. This is a time of profound disillusionment and alienation when a person struggles to go on in faith and looks for a way to renew commitment. Decisions about staying or leaving the community should be postponed until equilibrium has been regained and the choices are clear.

In the last stage people have made the major transition from "the community for me" to "me for the community." There is new freedom to participate in community life for the sake of God's reign rather than personal needs. In so doing, members have more realistic expectations about the personal sacrifice required. They recognize life in Christian community as their destiny. Their evident creative energy draws others into the community's life. These communities are free to grow or fail. Their security doesn't lie in succeeding, but in doing the will of God as they understand it.

M. Scott Peck, a psychologist and author of *The Different Drum*, has established a foundation for the encouragement of community life. He defines community as a group of two or more people who have been able to transcend their differences, regardless of their diversity in social, spiritual, educational, ethnic, economic, or political backgrounds, to achieve common goals. He sees the process of community building as time-consuming and arduous, requiring personal commitment and sacrifice. But he notes that after a group has become a community it can be a remarkably effective decision-making body prepared to take on such tasks as lobbying against the arms race, procuring increased services to the poor, or reinvigorating a parish or government agency. Peck identifies the following stages in community development:

- *Pseudo-community:* During this stage conflict is avoided, individual differences denied, and feelings hidden.

- *Chaos:* Differences and conflicts surface and there is a major effort to convert the other to one's point of view to restore unity. This stage is potentially the refiner's fire.

- *Emptiness:* This stage is the most crucial in forming true community. The group sacrifices its efforts to control others, lowers its expectations, and begins to embrace and celebrate individual differences.

- *True Community:* Falling in love again. This stage is characterized by feelings of joy and sorrow at the same time. Once the efforts to convert and heal others have been abandoned, much healing and conversion take place and the community is ready to take on its mission.[36]

Peck's summary observation is that communities have to go through these cycles or seasons over and over again during the process of life together.

The concept of life and death cycles in community life offered by Sr. Pat Brockman of the New Jerusalem Community provides a liberating perspective on the experience of a community in conflict. All communities, no matter where in the world they are located, go through a foundation period where they discover what is unique about themselves. They identify an establishing gift or charism, which may be anything. In the case of Community Covenant it was the call to give shelter to anyone in need. After the foundation period a community goes through a season of expansion in which its beliefs or vision is articulated and formalized so that people can be brought into membership. During this period the community norms are established and the membership covenant is formed, whether it is written or assumed. In any case there is a body of beliefs that is held in common and a sense of common direction held by all. Assumptions, dreams, and long-term mission goals are shared. There is a prevailing sense of unity as the community enters into what may be a long or a short season of stabilization.

Then the disintegration cycle begins. There is a breakdown of unity as soon as people begin to doubt the original vision and structures. The prevailing mood is that things are no longer working. In the stages of doubt, in contrast with the earlier stages of belief, the group moves from what is called operational doubt, which means that they no longer believe that the structures or organization of the community are working, to faith doubt, ethical doubt, and absolute doubt. This is a process that expresses the different levels of trust that are breaking down. During this process members begin to question everything they have previously held to be true, including the covenant. They begin to question the beliefs of others in a way that makes trust impossible, and finally the atmosphere becomes so filled with suspicion, judgment, and doubt that they must ask whether they still belong in the community. The breakdown period is the critical period in which the community will either die or be reborn.

### Difficult Transitions

One of the issues that brings people into crisis in community is the question of decision-making power. People must have a sense of participation in the decisions a community makes in order to feel empowered. This dynamic is directly related to the leadership style adopted by various communities. Communities that function with authoritarian leadership are more vulnerable to dissatisfied members and revolt than those that practice either consultative or enabling leadership styles. In some cases the death and rebirth of a community may be directly related to the leadership question.

A community may start out with a strong charismatic pastor. This style may be very effective, but eventually leadership changes or people begin to be dissatisfied by their lack of participation in major community decisions. Some people respond enthusiastically to being more included in decision making and others are deeply distressed. If a community can step back from strong emotion and study what is taking place in its life, it may be able to move into a new form of leadership and decision making that is empowering for all. The pascal mystery of Christ's life, death, and resurrection can be a paradigm of community life. When communities die, they die with Christ, and if they are reborn, they are reborn in Christ. When the Montana community lost its founder and struggled to regain an identity, it was being challenged as all communities are to let go of the old security and wait for the new.

Many communities die fighting. They refuse to let go of the old and accept change. The experience of a community in chaos is like being in a dark tunnel, but as death and dying experts have discovered, often those who return from a near-death experience report that they were being drawn toward a very bright light. The point at which many communities despair and break up or experience a significant loss of members is the very moment when they may be on the threshold of renewal. The death of the old vision and the birth of the new can be a refining experience bringing the community into a richness they never dreamed possible.

Some years ago the Church of the Saviour made a very difficult transition into what they described as their new land. They had grown too large to be effectively pastored and discipled within one church. After a year-long process of discussion, reflection, and retreat, involving many members of the community, seven sister communities emerged, each led by a different member of the church. They crossed over into their new land having gone down into death with Christ to be raised to new life with him. The church still has much to learn about this critical transition, which is the key to saying yes to life and taking our next steps into the promised land. Acknowledging endings and celebrating new beginnings may point the way.

# 8. Rooted and Grounded in Love
## Gifts and Healing in Community Life

> I pray that, according to riches of his glory [God] may grant that you be strengthened in your inner being with power through his Spirit, and that Christ may dwell in your hearts through faith, as you are being rooted and grounded in love. I pray that you may have the power to comprehend, with all the saints, what is the breadth and length and height and depth, and to know the love of Christ.
>
> — Ephesians 3:16–18

Wherever the discovery and the exercising of gifts for ministry are taking place within the church today people are being made whole. There will be evidence of spiritual energy and power by which people's lives are in the process of being transformed and healed. These dynamics of community life may be understood in two ways. First, the process of giving and receiving forgiveness has a profoundly healing effect on people. Second, discovering one's particular gifts and talents and using those gifts in the service of others help people to understand their purpose in life.

The way in which the identification of individual gifts within a church releases powerful new energy for service is a mysterious dynamic of community life. But the spiritual energy and power that is released when people are discovering and using their gifts clearly empower people to move beyond fears and insecurities and to offer themselves to the community and world in confidence. An example from a community-based health care program in Kenya is articulated by a woman from the Kaumoni village who says, "Before I was nothing. Now I am a community health worker." The secret of this empowerment seems to lie in teaching people to exercise their gifts for others rather than for personal gain. In the context of Christian community, gifts function differently from the self-centeredness that focuses on having power over others.

The connection between being healed and pursuing the service of others has been clearly expressed in the calling of the prophet Isaiah. Describing his vision of seeing God, he says,

> And I said "Woe is me! I am lost, for I am a man of unclean lips, and I live among a people of unclean lips; yet my eyes have seen the King, the Lord of hosts!"
>
> Then one of the seraphs flew to me, holding a live coal that had been taken from the altar with a pair of tongs. The seraph touched my mouth with it and said, "Now that this has touched your lips, your guilt has departed and your sin is blotted out."
>
> Then I heard the voice of the Lord saying, "Whom shall I send, and who will go for us?"
>
> And I said, "Here am I; send me !" (Isa. 6:5–8)

In a single moment Isaiah sees his need to be forgiven and made whole. But his sense of unworthiness is overshadowed by God's purpose for him. In God's touch he is forgiven, restored to wholeness, and called into ministry. The dimension that is often left out in sermons preached in many churches is that we need to be healed to respond effectively to God's call. Forgiveness empowers a person to respond to God's call to go to the people in mission and service. In the New Testament, the word "salvation" is used interchangeably with the word for healing. The discovery and use of one's gifts in community is part of the process of experiencing both healing and salvation. By making use of the gifts of everyone in the community the church can have a more vital presence in the world.

Spiritual gifts are those gifts or graces that have been entrusted to a person for the benefit of the whole community of the church. They often reflect a person's instinctive abilities, but they find their fulfillment when they are used for the enrichment of the corporate life of the church. Any community depends, whether consciously or not, on the exercising of a multitude of spiritual gifts for its life. Without the presence of these spiritual gifts a community ceases to exist. These gifts include the commonly understood and publicly recognized services associated with churches such as preaching, teaching, administration, and music. They also include less recognized gifts that might be called servanthood or support services within community life, such as providing help for people through transportation, grocery shopping, laundry, etc. And further, there are the controversial and often misunderstood gifts like prophecy, speaking in tongues, and healing. Whatever gift we are describing, 1 Corinthians 12 makes it clear that everyone has a gift to offer the body and further that they are all essential to the community's health. And in 2 Corinthians 14:1, we are advised to earnestly desire the spiritual gifts.

## One Body, Many Members

We may not think of ourselves as uniquely gifted. In fact this kind of talk may give rise to some discomfort. But a true understanding of our spiritual gifts is healing, for it is evidence that we have been created to be a part of something larger than ourselves. Our gift belongs not only to ourselves, but to God and to the community.

Paul chose the body analogy to illustrate the organic interdependence that is needed and intended within the church if it is to be a healing community in its own life and in the world. This metaphor may not accurately describe the reality in many churches, but it is a cornerstone for how we must understand the transformation of the institutional church into healing communities.

The body analogy, like other images of the church, describes a living, breathing organism composed of as many parts as there are members. This group of people, knitted together by the spirit of God, is the living reminder of God in Christ on this earth. In some theologies, the witness of the church is a major tenet of faith. In any case, being part of the church is not meant to be the casual action it has become in many parts of the world today, where church membership indicates more about one's social connections than anything else.

How can the church recover its power in people's lives? Perhaps by inviting people to come under the discipline of a common life, as one does in intentional church communities. In this approach all of people's lives, their talents and abilities, become part of the richness of community life. In this way, people whose identity rests solely in their position can be encouraged to offer themselves to the community in simple but necessary services. This can be a liberating transition and is certainly one aspect of what is meant in the conversion that calls people to new life in the first place.

The Church of the Saviour in Washington, D.C., is a very effective embodiment of discovering and using spiritual gifts for the good of others. Within each small group called a mission group, each person's gift is identified and put into service. These gifts go beyond those listed in 1 Corinthians 12. Each person's gift is given a name and that person is responsible for using it on behalf of the group. The practice of identifying people's special gifts takes place every year and is vital to keeping the mission group alive. Examples of spiritual gifts identified in their community include:

- *Moderator:* One who enables the group to keep focused on its overall vision of the church and of the world. The person exhibiting this gift has the ability to call forth gifts in others, prepare agenda and conduct the group meetings.

- *Spiritual Director:* One who accompanies other persons on their spiritual journey through listening, prayer, and holding them accountable to the agreed-on disciplines.

- *Shepherd:* One who teaches those who are exploring membership about the community and answers questions about the process.

- *Pastor/Prophet:* One who exercises the ability to call the group's attention to critical social issues and who also cares for the interrelationships within the group.

- *Visionary:* One who sees a larger picture and can call the group to respond.

- *Ecumenist:* One who carries the concern for the world church and its various local expressions into the life of the mission group.

- *Worship Leader:* One who prepares and leads the community in worship.

- *Celebrator:* One who calls the group to play and to celebrate.[37]

Describing their experience with identifying and using gifts to enrich the community's life, a member of the Wellspring mission group of the Church of the Saviour says:

> We have experienced over and over again the wonderful energy that comes to an individual and to a group when this teaching [Gifts] is taken seriously. Using this solid foundation (1 Corinthians 12 and Ephesians 4), we have been led to exciting creativity in naming a wide variety of gifts that work together to build group life and bring us all more fully into faithfulness as God's people.... We find that very intentional work in all these named areas by each member of the group is crucial if we are to continue to be faithful in our own personal inward journey and our mission. It is sometimes very difficult, but it always brings a measure of growth with deep joy.[38]

### Gifted Communities

Whether or not this particular list of spiritual gifts strikes a responsive chord, it is important to determine in our own context how we might take the Corinthians teaching on gifts seriously. I was raised in the church, but I never thought of myself as having a unique contribution to make to its life until I found the Church of the Saviour. One of the most significant discoveries of my adult life has been the realization that I have a God-given gift that is needed by the church if it is to bring healing to the nations. So does anyone who is a member of the church anywhere in the world. To this end Gordon Cosby has said in his *Handbook for Mission Groups:*

> The gift conferred by the holy spirit upon the new person in Christ is not a vague, general propensity, but a specific power or capacity peculiar to an individual, to be exercised for the good of the group. The failure to

take this teaching seriously is the cause of the apathy and ineffectiveness in the Christian church of our time.[39]

For this reason, it may be helpful to illustrate how broad and yet how specific spiritual gifts may be. We once asked our community in Montana to participate in a gift-inventory. We asked everyone in the community to respond to the following questions:

- How do you presently understand God's call on your life?

- What are your specific talents?

- What gifts are you most able to offer the community at this time?

The responses people shared were amazing in their variety. We all came together in the sanctuary and spent an evening talking about our gifts in smaller groups; we discussed how we were putting these gifts to use within community life, as well as what was preventing us from offering them to each other. Afterward, one of the pastors catalogued the gifts. Here are examples of spiritual gifts that include and expand on those listed in 1 Corinthians.

- the gift of teaching, as in leading Bible study

- retreat leadership

- teaching children art

- tutoring

- spiritual direction

- prophetic witness for justice

- music and worship leadership

- carrying the vision of the community

- ministering to emotionally disturbed children

- hospitality

- liturgical drama and dance

- contemplative prayer

- counseling

- prayer for inner healing

- listener

- reconciler in the community

- inter-faith dialogue

- spiritual friendship

- compassion

- peacemaker in global context

- marriage advocacy

- support for singleness

- administration

- ministry to handicapped persons

- faithfulness

- discernment

- servanthood, i.e., general helpfulness to whatever need arises (provide transportation, housecleaning, shopping and meals for those in need)

Perhaps in this list of gifts we can see that it is because they have been given for the use of the common good that they are distinguished from ordinary talents and abilities. Individually the gifts are not sufficient to create community. But when offered together in concert they express an astonishing breadth and completeness. I have heard it said that each community has the gifts it needs to minister and to maintain itself in whatever combination of people belongs to its life. However, in many churches one sees only a few highly visible gifted people carrying the life of the community. Can it really be because so few people are gifted, or is it more likely that many people have not yet discovered that they have a specific spiritual gift so that they can support the ministry of the church in a particular way?

So few Christians think of themselves as having a gift that is needed by the church to accomplish the work of

God that healing communities need to be places where this discovery can take place. It is also necessary to examine the reasons that keep people from offering themselves and their gifts to the life of the church. When we asked our community to talk about gifts, several people said that their own need to be healed was so great that they could not see what their gift might be, nor did they feel the energy to give themselves to the church's life in the midst of their pain. Certainly there are times when everyone will be incapacitated by grief. Paradoxically, it is often when we offer ourselves in the midst of our pain that we may find ourselves being made whole.

I have a friend who is a hospital chaplain in India who often refers to the "making-whole movement of God." This is a very apt description of the mission of the church. We are all called to find our place in the making-whole movement of God. Whatever blocks us from discovering and exercising our spiritual gifts must be understood and challenged.

# Conclusion: What Makes a Church a Healing Community?

> We seek within this riot of notes
> The gentle sounds
> That form a minor symphony
> To heal our wounds.
>
> At first, perhaps, life is an opus
> Of tragic wails —
> But then, if we attend to the theme,
> A form prevails.
>
> And from the mad cacophony
> That wreck'd our soul
> Emerges the sparse ecstatic song
> That makes us whole.
>
> — Charles Doss, prisoner,
> in *The Church Herald*

In May of 1990, a seminar on Christian Perspectives on Health, Healing, Wholeness, and Suffering was held at the Bossey Conference Center of the World Council of Churches. During ten days together, more than forty people from different regions of the world shared their experiences of what creates a healing community in the church. Although it was apparent that all communities do not look alike — that they exist for many different pastoral and prophetic reasons  including political action, health care, or prayer and contemplation — the group agreed that a healing community incorporates most of these characteristics:

1. *Commitment:* Communities cannot exist without a high level of commitment to membership. Whether or not a community has a formal covenant, there is always a deliberate process of becoming a member of the community.

2. *Discipleship:* Discipleship takes place in membership classes, small groups, and spiritual direction. These are all ways of communicating how the community understands its mission as God's people in this world. Some communities make use of formal spiritual directors or pairing with another community member to focus on spiritual growth and points of struggle.

3. *Journey Inward/Journey Outward:* Healing communities are involved in some aspect of the inward and outward spiritual journey. This means that they are nurturing inward spiritual growth in members through disciplines like prayer, reading and studying Scripture, and the keeping of a journal, and by challenging members to take the outward journey of response to the needs of the larger society.

4. *Small Groups:* Working, praying, and sharing in small groups is another characteristic of a healing community. These groups provide a context to be known intimately. There is clearly a special power in sharing our journey with other believers who can mediate God's forgiveness and acceptance in response to people's life stories.

5. *Telling Our Story:* A healing community is a place where one is free to tell his or her life story to people who are committed to accepting it in the spirit of Christ. It is a place where one learns to speak and to listen to another, especially to the isolating feelings of pain and anger that prevent fellowship. In some communities, this takes the form of sharing a spiritual autobiography during the process of becoming a member.

6. *Acceptance:* Theologian Paul Tillich said, "You are accepted by that which is greater than you. Simply accept the fact that you are accepted." Healing communities learn to value each member's unique personality as well as to make a place for those whom society finds unacceptable. They are challenged to accept theological differences within the community. Experience in life together has taught that it is often those who seem most limited by illness or handicap or those with discordant views who have the most to give the community.

7. *Corporate Life:* The emphasis on the common good that is expressed in community life is an important corrective to the self-centered living that dominates many industrialized nations. It teaches the members to care deeply for others and provides a sense of being a member of the global village that leads many communities to respond in concrete ministries of justice.

8. *Worship:* It is in corporate worship that music and Scripture take on new meaning and bind the community to-

gether in a common purpose. Worship is a living reminder that God is at the center of all healing. The celebration of the Eucharist is a central event where members are empowered to forgive each other and renew their vision of ministry. Some form of praying for healing among the members takes place.

9. *Alternative Leadership:* There are many different forms of leadership present in healing communities depending on the communion they represent. Leaders often emerge or are chosen on the basis of spiritual gifts rather than by official channels. Even those communions that accept a hierarchy between priests and laity, and women and men, usually have an expanded leadership team that draws on the gifts of many rather than a few. In many communities there is a commitment to lay leadership.

10. *Surviving Conflict:* Healing communities must learn to survive conflict by finding ways to reconcile the inevitable rifts that arise over personality, theological differences, and mission priorities, and to find in the chaos the seeds of new life.

11. *Trust:* Healing communities depend on trust, trust that our ultimate security in life rests in God and trust in the integrity of another person's experience. There has never been a time when the world had greater need of those people and those communities who know how to treat another person's life as holy ground — to bury their capacity to destroy in favor of creating communities that promote life and health for all.

12. *Time:* A member of our Bossey seminar who is the chaplain of a hospice outside Geneva reminded our group that building healing communities requires time. One cannot be in a hurry, for all the characteristics of community life depend on a new definition of how to be the church and require a radical reorientation of one's values. It takes time to build trusting relationships and it takes time to make a difference in this world.[40]

The Scriptures say that faith is the presence of things hoped for but not always seen. Building healing communities is an act of faith. We can not always see where our efforts will lead us and it is very costly to give one-self without reservation. But that is what it requires to transform the life of ordinary church congregations into healing communities. Human effort is not enough. We need God's Spirit blowing the breath of life into our midst. These characteristics of community life gleaned from churches throughout the world offer a place to begin the journey.

The topic of healing community is one about which there are more questions than answers. The mission in the writing of this book has been to say that Christians belong in community whatever the cost. Finally all the examples and characteristics must become personally compelling. We each need to find our place in the making-whole movement of God.

The question we need to ask ourselves is this: How can I participate in creating a healing community in my church?

# Appendix:
# A Service of Healing
# from the World Council of Churches

*Opening Prayer (sung by choir)*

*Opening Sentences (all standing)*

Leader:    God's perfect law revives the soul;
God's word makes wise the simple;
God's clear commands rejoice the heart;
God's light the eye enlightens.

All:    Lord who can tell the secret faults
that have dominion over me?
Hold back thy servant from self-will
and break its power to bind me.

May all I think and all I say
be now acceptable to you,
my Rock and my Redeemer.

*(Ps. 19:7–14)*

**SANCTUS**

P. Sosa, Argentina

Holy...
My heart, my heart adores you,
My heart knows how to say to you —
Holy are you Lord.

*Collect*

Leader:  Almighty God,
whose Son Jesus Christ
was tempted as we are,
yet without sin:
give us grace to discipline ourselves
in obedience to your Spirit;
and, as you know our weakness,
so may we know your power to save;
through Jesus Christ our Lord.

All:  Amen.

Hymn:  "O Christ, the Healer, We Have Come"

## O CHRIST, THE HEALER, WE HAVE COME

Fred Pratt Green          W. Walker, Southern Harmony

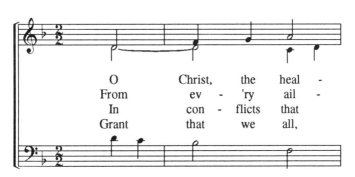

O          Christ,     the     heal -
From       ev - 'ry     ail -
In         con - flicts   that
Grant      that       we      all,

er   we  have   come          To    pray  for
ment flesh  en - dures          Our   bod - ies
de - stroy  our    faith,        We    rec - og -
made one   in     faith,        In    your com-

health,  to     plead   for  friends.        How
clam - or       o     be  freed;          Yet
nize   the      world's dis - ease;        Our
mu - ni      - ty    may  find             The

can   we   fail      to     be   re - stored When
in    our  hearts   we   would con - fess  That
com - mon life      de - clares our   ills.   Is
whole-ness that,    en - rich - ing   us,   Shall

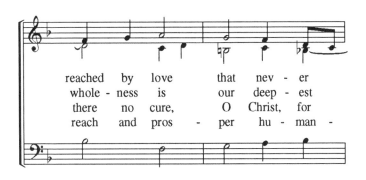

reached   by   love      that   nev - er
whole - ness  is      our   deep - est
there     no   cure,     O   Christ,  for
reach     and  pros  -  per   hu - man -

ends?
need.
these?
kind.

Words by Fred Pratt Green, reproduced by permission of
Stainer & Bell Ltd, London, England.   Setting copyright © 1972 CONTEM-
PORARY WORSHIP 4: Hymns for Baptism and Holy Communion.
Reprinted by permission of Augsburg Fortress.

*Prayer of Thanksgiving and Confession*

Leader: The Apostle Paul wrote:

In my inner being I delight in God's law but I see another law at work in the members of my body, waging war against the law of my mind and making me a prisoner of the law of sin at work within my members.

Who will rescue me from this body of death? Thanks be to God through Jesus Christ our Lord!

All: Thanks be to God through Jesus Christ our Lord!

*(Romans 7:15–18b, 22–25)*

Leader: O God
Giver of Life
Bearer of Pain
Maker of Love

We thank you that
you are able to accept in us
what we cannot even acknowledge;
you are able to name in us
what we cannot bear to speak of;
you are able to hold in your memory
what we have tried to forget;
you are able to hold out to us
the glory that we cannot conceive.

Have mercy on us this day,
Reconcile us through your cross
to all that we have rejected in ourselves,
that we may find no part of your creation
to be alien or strange to us,
and that we ourselves may be made whole.

Through Jesus Christ our Lord.

Amen.

## ENTRY OF THE WORD (standing)

Christopher Walker: England

A - le - lu - ia    A - le - lu - ia

A-le-lu-ia    A-le-lu-ia    A-le-lu-ia

A-le-lu-ia    A-le-lu-ia    A - le - lu - ia

© 1980/1991 Christopher Walker. All rights reserved.

*Reading*

They arrived on the other side of Lake Galilee, at the territory of the Gerasenes. As soon as Jesus got out of the boat he was met by a man who came out of the burial caves. This man had an evil spirit in him and lived among the graves. Nobody could keep him tied with chains any more; many times his feet and hands had been tied, but every time he broke the chains, and smashed the irons on his feet. He was too strong for anyone to stop him. Day and night he wandered among the graves and through the hills, screaming and cutting himself with stones.

He was some distance away when he saw Jesus; so he ran, fell on his knees before him, and screamed in a loud voice, "Jesus, Son of the Most High God! What do you want with me? For God's sake, I beg you, don't punish me!" (He said this because Jesus was saying to him, "Evil spirit, come out of this man!")

So Jesus asked him, "What is your name?"

The man answered, "My name is 'Mob' — there are so

many of us!" And he kept begging Jesus not to send the evil spirits out of that territory.

A large herd of pigs was near by, feeding on the hillside. The spirits begged Jesus, "Send us to the pigs, and let us go into them." So he let them. The evil spirits went out of the man and went into the pigs. The whole herd — about two thousand pigs in all — rushed down the side of the cliff into the lake and were drowned.

The men who had been taking care of the pigs ran away and spread the news in the town and among the farms. They came to Jesus and saw the man who used to have the mob of demons in him. He was sitting there, clothed and in his right mind; and they were all afraid.

*(Mark 5:1–15)*

### *Response to the Word*

As with scarlet and fine linen thy church is adorned with the blood of thy martyrs in all the world, and through them she cries aloud to Thee, O Christ our God: have compassion on thy people, grant peace to thy flock, and to our souls great mercy.

### *Symbolic Action — Prayers for Healing*

Jesus asked the demoniac his name — in order to understand his character, his essence. To reply that his name was Legion, immediately explained to Jesus the internal state of the man's life. He had no control, he was not one, but many, all the driving forces within him were at war with each other.

Jesus invites us to name the contradictions inside of us, which we cannot control.

We stand for justice —
    but enjoy the fruits of injustice.

We are concerned for the preservation of creation —
    but participate in its destruction.

Like the Gerasene demoniac, we recognize the conflict within ourselves toward Jesus; on the one hand rushing up to him, and on the other hand, begging him to go.

As the Apostle Paul testified:

> I do not understand what I do
> For what I want to do I do not do
> but what I hate, I do.
>
> For I have the desire to do what is good
> but I cannot carry it out.

Let us in silence before God name the contradictions inside of us.

*(Silence)*

In the ancient tradition of the church you are invited to come forward to pray for healing; the healing of your spirit and/or body, or for the healing of someone else, and then to receive from one of the celebrants a blessing.

94

## RECESSIONAL SONG:
## NADA TE TURBE (Santa Teresa de Jesús)

Music: Jacques Berthier

Na - da te tur - be, na - da te es - pan - te,

quien a Dios tie - ne na - da le fal - ta.

Na-da te tur-be, na-da te es-pan-te, só-lo Dios bas - ta.

Let nothing trouble you, let nothing frighten you: whoever has God lacks nothing. God alone is enough.

Nichts beunruhige dich, nichts ängstige dich: Wer Gott hat, dem fehlt nichts. Gott allein genügt.

Que rien ne te trouble, rien ne t'effraie: qui a Dieu ne manque de rien. Seul Dieu suffit.

© Ateliers et Presses de Taizé, 71250 Taizé community, France

*Benediction*

May the blessing of God who risked everything for our sake, the blessing of the Christ-child who releases in us new visions of hope, and the blessing of the Holy Spirit who guides and directs us into new forms of obedience, be with us all.

# Notes

**Introduction / O Healing River, Send Down Your Waters:
In Search of Healing Community within the Church**

1. "Health in Search of Wholeness: The Journey of the Medical Mission Sisters," *CMC Contact*, no. 119 (April 1991): 4.

2. Abigail Rian Evans, M.Div., Ph.D., "A Prescription for Health," *Presbyterian Church USA*, September 1985.

**1 / To Become Healing Communities:
The Christian Medical Commission Challenges the Churches**

3. Adapted from the CMC report *Healing and Wholeness: The Church's Role in Health* (Geneva: World Council of Churches, 1990), 1–4. Unless otherwise noted, all citations in this chapter are taken from this report.

4. Ibid., 9.

5. Ibid., 19.

6. Ibid., 15–16.

7. Ibid., 7–8.

8. Ibid., 13.

9. Ibid., 14.

10. Bernie S. Siegel, M.D., *Love, Medicine and Miracles* (New York: Harper & Row, 1986), cover.

11. Abraham Verghese, M.D., from a paper presented at a symposium on Faith and Healing, February 1980.

12. *Healing and Wholeness,* 36–37.

**2 / Healing Community in Global Perspective**

13. Bruce Menning, "Action/Reflection Paper on Latin American Base Ecclesial Communities," May 1990, 19.

14. Jether Pereira Ramalho, "Church Base Communities: An Ecumenism Made by the People," in *WCC/CCPD for a Change,* 1990, 17.

15. Roberto Bolton G., "Unsuspected Horizons: Ordinary People Reading the Bible," in *WCC/CCPD for a Change,* 1990, 16.

16. Wanda Deifelt, "Brazilian Women: The Religious is Political," *Daughters of Sarah* (March/April 1991): 16–17.

17. Sr. Anne Moran, M.M.M., in "Basic Christian Communities," *MMM Magazine*.

18. Sarah Summers, M.M.S., and Mary Pawath, M.M.S., "Health in a Search for Wholeness: The Journey of the Medical Mission Sisters," *CMC Contact,* no. 119 (April 1991): 5.

19. Quoted in ibid., 8.

20. Adapted from Gene Beerens, "Liberation of Captives Closer to Home"; published as "Who Listens to Whom?" in *One World* (May 1991): 4.

21. Ibid., 5.

22. Adapted from Benjamin Pulimood, M.D., "Healing Ministry and Ashiramams," *Christian Medical Journal of India* (July–September 1986): 40–41.

23. A. C. Oomen, "Healing, Wholeness and Salvation" (New York: Vellore Christian Medical College Board, 1980).

24. Sister Mary MacDonald, "Toward a Christian Ministry of Healing in Mararoko," *CMC Contact,* no. 119 (April 1991): 9.

### 3 / Biblical Origins of Healing Community

25. Gabriel Moran, quoted in a lecture on Christian Community by Patrick Granfield, Catholic University, Washington, D.C.

26. *Wellspring,* newsletter of the Church of the Saviour, March 1985, 3.

27. Richard Rohr, O.F.M., in *Wellspring,* March 1985, with permission of *Sojourners* magazine.

28. From the "Statement of Purpose" brochure of the Community of Communities, circulated privately to its members.

### 4 / You Have Been Christ to Me: The Story of Community Covenant Church

29. "The Servant Song" was composed by Richard Gillard. The words "Beloved" and "family" are substituted for "brother" by our congregation.

### 5 / Pressing On: The Discipline of Life Together

30. Membership disciplines articulated by Community Covenant Church, Missoula, Montana.

31. The Church of the Saviour is located at 2025 Massachusetts Ave., Washington, DC 20036; tel. (202) 387-1617.

32. Membership disciplines articulated by Community Covenant Church, Missoula, Montana.

**6 / The Death of the Dream: Conflict in Community Life**

33. David Anderson and John Schramm, *Dance in Steps of Change* (New York: Thomas Nelson, 1970), 13–14.
34. Andrew Elsen, letter to the pastoral team of Community Covenant Church, Missoula, Montana.

**7 / Faith to Go Out with Good Courage:
Seasons of Community Life**

35. From a letter to friends of Bartimaeus Community, 1984.
36. M. Scott Peck, *The Different Drum* (London: Simon & Schuster, 1987). Peck is the founder of the Foundation for Community Encouragement, 7616 Gleason Road, Knoxville, TN 37919.

**8 / Rooted and Grounded in Love:
Gifts and Healing in Community Life**

37. *Wellspring* newsletter, September 1986. The identification of spiritual gifts in use at the Church of the Saviour, Washington, D.C., is discussed further in Gordon Cosby's *Handbook for Mission Groups* (Waco, Tex.: Word Books, 1975).
38. Myra Flood, *Wellspring* newsletter, September 1986.
39. Gordon Cosby, *Handbook for Mission Groups,* 91.

**Conclusion / What Makes a Church a Healing Community?**

40. These characteristics reflect the discussion held in small groups at the Bossey meeting on "Health, Healing, Wholeness and Suffering," May 1990, but have been expanded by the author.

# Suggestions for Further Reading

Bonhoeffer, Dietrich. *Life Together*. New York: Harper and Row, 1954.

Cosby, Gordon. *Handbook for Mission Groups*. Waco, Tex.: Word Books, 1975.

Crawley, Gwen, and David Zuverink. *Creating Communities of Health, Healing and Wholeness*. Louisville, Ky.: Presbyterian Church USA, 1989.

Gish, Arthur G. *Living in Christian Community*. Scottsdale, Pa.: Herald Press, 1979.

Granberg-Michaelson, Karin. *In the Land of the Living: Health Care and the Church*. Grand Rapids, Mich.: Zondervan, 1984.

Nouwen, Henri J. M. *Reaching Out: The Three Movements of the Spiritual Life*. Garden City, N.Y.: Doubleday, 1975.

O'Connor, Elizabeth. *Letters to Scattered Pilgrims*. New York: Harper & Row, 1982.

O'Connor, Elizabeth. *The New Community*. New York: Harper & Row, 1982.

Peck, M. Scott. *The Different Drum*. New York: Simon and Schuster, 1987.

Sine, Tom. *The Mustard Seed Conspiracy*. Waco, Tex.: Word Books, 1981.

Vanier, Jean. *Community and Growth*. Ramsey, N.J.: Paulist Press, 1979.